"It was, as expec... ...ng true and so mu...

Leader of C...

"Exceptional. A g... ...to change. The book will be a catalyst."
**Nikki Rucci,
Pastor at Rivercity Family Church,
Brisbane, Australia**

"An essential guide for leaders to reflect on how to create safe, fearless churches that truly reflect Christ."
**Pastor Ken Harrison,
Superintendent New Zealand Assemblies of God,
2003–2011**

BETTER THAN THIS

Creating safe, fearless church cultures in a complex world

Copyright © 2025 David Warren

The moral right of the author has been asserted.

Apart from any fair dealing for the purposes of research or private study, or criticism or review, as permitted under Copyright, Design and Patents Act 1998, this publication may only be reproduced, stored or transmitted, in any form or by any means, with prior permission in writing of the publishers, or in any case of the reprographic reproduction in accordance with the terms of licences issued by the Copyright Licensing Agency. Enquiries concerning reproduction outside these terms should be sent to the publishers.

PublishU Ltd

www.PublishU.com

Scripture from the Holy Bible, New International Version®, NIV®.

Copyright © 1973, 1978, 1984, 2011 by Biblica, Inc.™ Used by permission of Zondervan. All rights reserved worldwide.

All rights of this publication are reserved.

Thanks

I am deeply grateful to my family for travelling the journey with me. Their faithfulness, patience, gifts, integrity and character have motivated me to keep going and inspired me to write. Without them the story would never be there to be told let alone written. Thank you, Jayne, Becci, Sarah, Daniel, Heidi, Finley, Caleb and not least little Joel. You are all much loved.

Contents

Introduction

Boundaries

Part One: **Storytelling**

Chapter 1 Everything: Jesus Knew Everything About Her

Chapter 2 My Story of (Nearly) Everything

Chapter 3 The Romanian Story

Chapter 4 Sophie's Story

Chapter 5 The Story Through Leadership Eyes

Epilogue

Part Two: **Interludes**

Interlude 1 Theological Wisdom

Interlude 2 Psychological Safety

Interlude 3 Courageous Followership

Epilogue

Part Three: The New Story

Writing A New Story

Encore

Part Four: Jesus Shaped Cultures

Leadership and Culture

Voices That Challenge

Jesus: Wise, Safe and Courageous

Conclusion

About the Author

Introduction

I have always liked to influence people, organisations, churches and teams. I was often a team captain at school and was always dreaming of how I might do this or that in the Methodist Church I belonged to for 20 years.

My first community project was launched on the back of an idea concocted during a very boring sermon whilst sitting on a hard pew towards the back of a cold church. Most of the dreams have never materialised! When at Stoneleigh East Primary School, I loved the weekly free writing sessions we had. I created a football team with heroes, villains, coaches and managers. I filled many exercise books and the sessions kept the class quiet! My team always won the league even if we had to come from behind and beat our greatest rivals in the last match of the season. Now there's a surprise. Fifty-five years later the desire to influence and the creativity of writing have finally come together in this little manuscript. It has taken too long and a few very inadequate attempts along the way. I should have done better than that!

For all my life the church has been centre stage. It has been part of me. Most of the time it has been a happy relationship, sometimes challenging and fulfilling and always a privilege. I have met amazing people, seen extraordinary things and hopefully had a positive influence on a few folks and communities along the way. Over recent years my evangelical churchy world has been shaken by a series of scandals involving money, sex and power. Long hidden stories of abuse and control have been uncovered, and many brave people have spoken out. This book reflects the impact this has had not only on victims but also on my thinking and practice. The numerous stories, reports and articles I have listened to and read have saddened and shaken my thinking and even my faith. The more I investigate, the more it disturbs me. What has gone wrong? What part have I played? Have I believed in unwise theology and unhealthy leadership theory? This book is an attempt to answer some of my own questions, to have an influence and to make a positive difference. My new dream is that it will help people create churches that are safe and free from fear.

Boundaries

Stories are personal and sometimes the story holder doesn't want to share all the details of their story. It can be too personal or traumatic to do so. Many dates, names, details and locations have therefore been altered. Please don't try to be Poirot or Miss Marple. Stories will be told in first person and may or may not be a story about me (where I think it appropriate, I will let the reader know it is "me" speaking). Every story is real, and every story reflects real people in real time. I am deeply grateful to everyone who has helped by allowing me to tell their story. For some this has been an immensely courageous act.

My background (as you will soon discover) is largely shaped by being part of what has been labelled as the Pentecostal/Charismatic family. It is a big and colourful collection of leaders, groups, streams, spheres, families and tribes (or whatever the "in" term is). Theology and practice vary from one group to another, one church to another. I am very aware of the danger of generalisations and labels. Sometimes however this is difficult to avoid especially as definitions are often difficult (if not impossible) to tie down. One person's Apostle is another person's Prophet!

I will use the term "spiritual abuse". A troublesome phrase for some and profoundly traumatic for others. Some would rather avoid the term and lump stories into the category of psychological or emotional abuse. The Evangelical Alliance Theological Advisory Group states that spiritual abuse is a "seriously problematic term because of its own inherent ambiguity." The concern centres around potential discrimination, criminalisation and social cohesion. Other Christian research by ThirtyOne Eight and Lisa Oakley (2017) recognise spiritual abuse as requiring its own categorisation but not requiring "any additional criminalisation" (see reports by Evangelical Alliance and ThirtyOne Eight). Whilst recognising the nuances of this debate it seems clear to me that those who have suffered terribly from abusive practices in Christian settings can only describe the pain as abuse of their "soul" or "spirit". Christian belief has always understood the human being as a profound mix of body, mind and spirit. So, in what follows, I use the term "spiritual abuse" to describe a form of emotional and psychological abuse where there are patterns of behaviours described by definitions below. It isn't perfect but I hope readers will understand and not throw stones!

I will not say much about trauma or trauma-informed practice. I am no expert, and I felt it went beyond the scope of what I have felt free to share. If you have suffered from any kind of abuse, then trauma may not be too far away. I am sorry. I am sorry that my world has got it so wrong on far too many occasions.

I am happy to settle with either of the following definitions of spiritual abuse and I proceed with caution and in the hope that those who see things a bit differently will give grace.

"Spiritual abuse is a form of emotional and psychological abuse. It is characterised by a systematic pattern of coercive and controlling behaviour in a religious context. Spiritual abuse can have a deeply damaging impact on those who experience it. However, holding a theological position is not in itself inherently spiritually abusive, but misuse of Scripture, applied theology and doctrine is often a component of spiritually abusive behaviour."— ThirtyOne Eight and Lisa Oakley

"The word spiritual refers to something affecting a human spirit or soul. Abuse means to mistreat another, to deceive or do harm. When we use the word spiritual to describe abuse, we are talking about using that which is sacred — including God's Word — to control, misuse, deceive, or damage a person created in His image." — Diane Langberg

This is not a book primarily about spiritual abuse nor is it another, "How To Do Leadership" book. There are far too many of them around! This is my story and how it interacts with the stories of others. It paints a picture of a beautiful church scarred by a serious illness. The story reveals some of the symptoms of this illness and suggests what medication might be applied. The Interludes are the technical bit and will support the diagnosis making sure healthy medication is taken by us all. Part three aims to set the stage for a new story to be written, not by me but by you and all who read. It introduces several characters that need to be in the script. Part four delves a little more into leadership and the varied voices that are heard as we attempt to create and then act out the new story of healthy, safe, fearless churches. In this section we will turn and face the writer and director of it all: Jesus.

DAVID WARREN

Part One:
Storytelling

There is a well-known football chat show hosted by Robbie Savage and Chris Sutton called 6-0-6 on Radio 5 live. Opinions are strong as callers know more about complex tactics than the very best manager or player. Chris has developed a little catch phrase that he uses to point out when he feels the skill and character of a player doesn't quite match their action on the pitch (often rolling across the field screaming in pain after a minor touch on an ankle). "You are better than that," states Chris.

In recent years I have become increasingly concerned that my churchy world has often fallen far short of what we are called and designed to be. We have screamed "foul". I have been part of the problem so I write with trepidation as I know some folks are likely to label me a "hypocrite". I understand. I have fallen for some of the traps. I am sorry. I get it. At times I should have been better than that. I cannot change history but I can use it to help change the future.

Jesus Christ should always be centre stage in all church settings. We are part of His new creation and the church is empowered by the Spirit to be a new creation; people demonstrating the kingdom of righteousness, joy and peace to a needy world. As such she should be the safest, most beautiful, most creative gathering of people in the world. Fear has no place in the Church. I have come to the conclusion that we can do better than we have! Our character, speech and actions have not matched the message. We have fallen over and got ourselves very muddy and then made excuses. Some have understandably given us the red card as a result of our actions and many of their stories are now emerging.

We really are better than this!

We can only be and do better as we honestly talk about the issues and bring them into the light so that the best remedies can be applied. If we don't know what is wrong, we are unlikely to apply the right medication and may even make the disease far worse. I hope the stories shine light and the "interludes" can be used as effective healing balms. That is up to the reader to decide.

My hope is that we can also share enough wonderful stories to encourage you all, enough challenging stories to make you think and enough remedies to help you in your unique situation. The church really is the "multi-coloured wisdom of God" (Ephesians 3:10).

Together we can be so much better than this!

My class of 10 year old children had been captivated by Michael Morpurgo's, 'The Wreck of the Zanzibar' in which Laura's much-loved grandmother dies. A sensitive subject to chat through when so many of the class had elderly grandparents. We cannot hide death from our children forever. The challenge was to write the story of the funeral day from Laura's point of view. I will never forget reading one child's reflection to a group of sceptical parents. Nearly all shed tears as they listened. They too had been captivated by a story. It was one of those unforgettable moments.

Yuval Harari once said, "Storytelling is our superpower." This young lady's story blew away sceptical minds and emotions were touched. This was her superpower moment.

Stories make us laugh and cry, they challenge and they inspire. Handled badly, stories start wars and make people miserable. Handled well, stories create, invent and change people and places for the good of all. Your story defines you, makes you unique, shapes your thinking and impacts those around you. You are your story. Good, bad, painful or happy — your story will connect you to others or perhaps disconnect you from the world around you. It may just lead you to walk away from God and His church. You also have far more power to write your story than you may think. Abuse and trauma attempt to take away your ability and strength to write your story. Better to just let it all be and shrink back into a false me, a me that is far from the real you that hides beneath the pain.

Stories are also a mix of the mysterious and the certain. They can be comical and serious all at once. They are not a simple result of scientific processes and cannot be easily analysed and understood. Sometimes the very mystery of it all is the beauty of it. How come a lonely man on a cross has influenced the history of the world like no other? It's a mysterious good news story. A story well told is compelling and draws you into a new world. Michael Morpurgo is a genius story-teller and that young girl caught the bug!

This book is about stories; stories of joy, pain, hurt, sadness, strength and brilliance. It is about people who in their journey of faith have encountered systems, leaders and people who are also attempting to work out their own story. It is about my story and the interaction I have had with hundreds of people over 40 years of church leadership (alongside teaching, mentoring, parenthood and family). By definition it is not perfect: no people story is ever perfect. It struggles with faith, love, hope, the Bible and a church which at its best is a story of life giving grace but at its worst, a horror story of abuse, power and politics. Stories create love and start wars!

None of our stories are acted out in a vacuum. We interact with people, systems, creation, history, research, science and so much more. Often we don't realise that our story is a source for a new story of invention and creativity. I am currently sitting in Costa Coffee. When I started my leadership journey, Costa was just a few years old (launched in 1971). Someone somewhere knew that human beings were craving a "third place" where they could sit and tell their stories (in my case, "write" their story). Costa is now everywhere, along with Starbucks, Neros and numerous other brands.

As a Christian, my life has been wrapped up in another story. It is the biggest, most significant story of all. The Bible tells this story. My whole life has been influenced, challenged and changed by this story. Sometimes I have misunderstood it and handled it badly, but mostly (I hope) it has been a source of joy and significant positive change in the lives and communities that have interacted with my story. Others will have their stories and will fundamentally disagree with my version of the story. That is OK. We don't start verbal wars, but we live to learn.

The Bible is essentially the story of God's interaction with His creation. At the heart of it all is the shocking story of new creation launched through servanthood, suffering, death and resurrection, rather than power and politics. The cross remains foolishness to the wisest of fallen humanity. This extraordinary story of a real person called Jesus, in the right hands and empowered by servanthood, has created a better world. Education and health and many of the finest charities have been inspired by the Jesus story. Our culture has been shaped in ways that most of us cannot even begin to comprehend; not by politicians nor kings nor emperors nor philosophers but by Jesus. Sadly, the good news Jesus story has also been abused, manipulated and misused and as a result, people have suffered terribly. People have suffered because they've loved like Jesus whilst others have suffered because those who say they love Jesus have used His name and His story as a weapon.

Whilst this book seeks to tell stories that challenge the church and its leaders to be a bit more like the

Jesus story, it also recognises the huge challenges leaders face. It is all too easy to take sides and attack. I seek to provide some solutions that are rooted in research and experience that will help us to be wiser, clearer and kinder. As you will read, I was part of the problem as well as helping to be an answer. I regret many silly mistakes.

It is not a theological book (although there is some theology), it is not a leadership book (although there is some leadership thinking). I suspect it will raise more questions than answers, but isn't that what Jesus did when He told His stories? He raised questions that could only be answered as people allowed themselves to become part of His story. This is a story book and my hope is that as my very inadequate story is told, a few folks will enter into the story with me and listen and perhaps shed a few "change tears". A 10-year-old in a Nuneaton classroom did it. I hope I can. Perhaps after all these years, this will be my "superpower".

Chapter 1
Everything: Jesus Knew Everything About Her

Story-telling is an art form and John was an expert.

He has stories within stories and the genius is that it all comes together when "early in the morning on the first day of the week" Mary discovers an empty tomb. A new day and a new creation had begun. Light shone out of the darkness and the darkness couldn't overwhelm it. Darkness and light are important to John as they are to so many story-tellers. Darkness creates atmosphere and is often associated with fear, secrecy or danger. Nicodemus comes to Jesus in the dark of night, Judas leaves the room of friends at night and Annas — the high priest — tries Jesus at night. It is no coincidence that the story of a lone woman at a well takes place when the light was at its brightest and follows on from the dark approach by the powerful, religious scholar called Nicodemus.

The Samaritan "woman at the well" has been labelled by many as immoral, an adulterer and even a prostitute who needed to repent of her fallen ways. But note what John doesn't say. There is no mention of sex, repentance, adultery, promiscuity, sin or prostitution. Caryn Reeder writes, "These poor patterns of interpretation have created places where women can be abused... There are other ways to read John 4 that show women as something other than sexualised sinners."

In the days of Jesus, women could be educated and important. Her questions were well considered and her responses honest and astute. Yes, she was alone, invisible and clearly she faced the challenge of isolation. In our language she might well be considered as an "other". We are far too quick to label. What about the possibility of a very young woman (12–15 years old) being married off to a much older man? Women often outlived several husbands. Perhaps she was abandoned by men because of infertility? Maybe — just maybe — she was the victim of abuse. She certainly carried a complicated and troubled story, not just a water jar!

And then the "other" meets Jesus and her story becomes part of world history. He sees everything, breaks the religious rules and finds nothing to shame nor to condemn. Down come the barriers that history, religion and powerful unseen forces had built. Jesus is on His own, He is tired, He is the Son of God and He is thirsty and asks the "other" for a drink. Surely the Messiah could find water for Himself! The woman helps another human in need and is treated with respect and dignity.

Vulnerability, respect and dignity shine light into dark places.

At the time of writing, another story of abuse has emerged. Another pastor has resigned and then declares he is under attack and weaves a dark story which seeks to justify and blame. A victim of a complicated life is victimised again by someone who is supposed to be a Jesus person. No respect, no dignity, no vulnerability. A pastor becomes part of the darkness rather than a thirsty man in the midday sun!

She Told Jesus Everything

There is a reason why solitary confinement is used as a punishment. Humans need other humans. On our own we are lonely and loneliness is painful. Those of us who believe every human being is an image bearer of a triune God know that a solitary existence is also a spiritual disease. Those of us who were separated from family and friends during the COVID years believing a touch or a breath may spread disease will know something of that feeling of isolation and even fear. We walked on the other side of the road and were suspicious of anyone with a cough. For many, life was intolerably lonely.

The lady pushed through the crowds knowing full well that her condition meant enforced separation from family and friends. No hugs! Walk on the other side of the road just in case. She was unclean and a touch would make others unclean. Deep down she knew this new young prophet on the street had the answer and so she found a way to struggle through, reach out and touch. The touch was in fact one of healing not harm as most would have assumed. It was enough to heal and she blurts out her whole story. The words that followed were ones of hope, healing, dignity and respect; the cherry on top of the cake of physical healing. "Peace (Shalom) be with you." This lady had experienced little peace for 12 long years. She too was "othered" and she too met the man who knew everything, listened to everything and then changed everything. "Otherness" had pursued her but now peace enveloped her. Shalom.

Well-being, security and harmony. What treasures these are for any human being and especially for those who have suffered the opposite. Jesus people should be peace makers, not hurt creators. Sadly (as we shall find out) this is not always the case. Victims have often been isolated, felt unclean and unworthy.

"The young lady had given her very best over a number of years. Long hours, no pay, little reward or recognition. She had done it all for Jesus and loved being with her friends. With friends there is identity and fun even when the going gets tough. She finally had enough of the demand culture. 'I was devastated that the leadership told my gang to give me space and allow me to work things out on my own. 'Please do not contact, it is for her good." The church creates an 'other' and sends them into a lonely place" (Story of an intern and staff member).

Those who are called to be peacemakers can easily become the very ones who when in places of power, do more harm than good. Jesus was so much better than this!

Peter Told Them Everything That Had Happened

Sometimes God uses shock treatment to shake us out of our comfort zones or push us into new areas of service and mission. The Bible is full of such stories; as is history. Who could have imagined that this small, Jewish-rooted Jesus-following community would suddenly be called to serve the Gentile world? It would need fresh vision, a new calling and a very clear story to tell. This is exactly what happened to Peter. Vision. Calling. Story. It was shocking and exciting all at once. His mates back in Jerusalem wanted to know more as they had their concerns. Peter tells them the "whole story" (everything) and in response, they welcome the new day and add a demand, "care for the poor". It must have felt very familiar. Didn't Jesus extend grace to a Samaritan woman at a well and an unclean woman pushing through a crowd?

Good, healthy, wise, vulnerable shepherds must be able and willing to tell their story. How have we come to the point where we are convinced that God has spoken? Without the story, we create demand, control and there is no space for accountability. Peter shared His story with others and they all interacted with the wider story that was being acted out at the time. No secrets. No hidden agendas. Leaders must be able to tell the whole story and be open to advice, opinions, adjustment and even additional demands. Healthy accountability is the fruit of respect, dignity and vulnerability. It creates space for shalom.

Over the years I have heard and presented numerous

vision presentations. "The Lord" has spoken to me. We expect everyone to jump on board just because God has "told" the anointed leader. If we ask questions, then that can easily be interpreted as "not trusting your leaders", as they are the ones tasked with hearing from God. Could it be that some of us are in danger of creating a new form of priesthood that our forefathers fought to distance themselves from? Peter had heard from God. He had an amazing vision. He was secure enough to share his story and allow others to ask questions and add to his story. It really wasn't his story to tell in the first place.

When Everything Goes Wrong

I loved teaching children to write stories. There is so much hidden creativity in every little person. The best way to teach a story is to tell stories. Lots of them. 'Dogger' by Shirley Hughes is a great example of a story plot. All starts well, something terrible happens (Dogger is lost) and then there is the adventure journey until the problem is solved when Dogger is finally found at the school fête.

The Bible is a story. It starts in a garden, ends in a garden, but there are a whole lot of twists and turns between the two gardens (or is it really one?). There are times when everything seems to go very well and people live in peace, the widow and orphan are cared for and justice reigns. At other times everything goes terribly wrong. Those who were supposed to shine a light and display the beauty of their Creator too easily become the cause and source of darkness.

Time and time again God rescues and redeems through "heroes of faith" until, finally, the answer is ultimately revealed at the darkest moment when all seems lost. Then resurrection and a new creation dawns. There is light and hope for the whole of broken creation! This is the narrative into which many amazing, sad, triumphant, mysterious and wonderful stories are written and into which we are all drawn. We too can be light shiners or darkness creators. We can be the heroes or villains. The stories are brutally honest and sometimes those who were supposed to be the good guys turn out to be the bad guys. Leaders who were supposed to be good shepherds harm the sheep. Kings who were supposed to rule justly and humbly walk proudly and the widow and orphan suffer. The story really is quite dark at times.

Into all this mess God raises up voices that speak into the dark places. There is always hope and always a sense that all will end up well, but the adventure journey to peace will mean suffering and servanthood. Such strange tools to use to rescue Dogger! Some of the light-shining voices are called "prophets" and some suffered for speaking out and seeking justice. Jeremiah was one of these.

"Shepherds" was a term Jeremiah used to describe leaders in various positions of power and authority. "Sheep" (you and me) were supposed to be looked after, protected, fed and healed by these shepherds. Poor shepherding would lead to poorly, beaten, scattered sheep. Uncared for widows and orphans felt the brunt of the injustice. They were "othered". Jesus was the master Shepherd who gathered lost sheep and imparted peace. To speak peace but to act out injustice was the pinnacle of hypocrisy and mask-wearing.

What happens when shepherding goes wrong, when dignity, respect, transparency, accountability and care for the poor are twisted, manipulated and disregarded? Jeremiah saw it all and named it as it was. Those who were supposed to create safe places were abusing their power and roles and the sheep were scattered, bewildered and damaged.

"Among my people are the wicked,

Who lie in wait like men who snare birds,

And like those who set traps to catch people.

Like cages full of birds,

Their houses are full of deceit;

They have become rich and powerful.

The prophets prophecy lies,

The priests rule by their own authority.

They dress the wound of My people

As though it is not serious.

'Peace, peace,' they say,

When there is no peace" (Jeremiah 5:26, 31, 6:14).

We will look into specifics later, but for now it is enough to say that when the shepherds get it wrong, people suffer and sadly the stories told and the many yet to be told illustrate the horrors that follow when what should be the safest place becomes the abusive space.

In July 2022 the Pathfinder Report was published into serious allegations made by numerous attendees of Arise Church, New Zealand. The scandal hit the headlines and 545 official responses were submitted. Many more used social media to express their experiences. At the time when headlines were being made the Senior Pastor was due to speak at the Assembly of God (UK) national leadership conference (the influence of these mega-shepherds is huge). The report described a catalogue of abusive and controlling behaviours leading the report to state that "people have experienced significant harm through their involvement with Arise Church". Issues included extravagant spending by pastors, bullying, sexual harassment, "outbursts of anger" leading people to feeling "anxious about future interactions" and much more. Read back over Jeremiah 5 and 6 (and other passages) and see in those old words a modern-day story of shepherds scattering and abusing sheep for their own gain. What is declared as a place of peace becomes a place of harm to many.

A poem I received from a victim in another setting describes the confusion, fear and shame when everything goes so horribly wrong and peace is shattered:

"Would it be easier? Would it be easier for you, if he had raped me?

If I had been younger than 15?

If I had recorded us together?

Would that help you to know how much to punish, and how much to sweep away, down play. If he had touched me, would you have known what to call him?

A paedophile, a criminal, a predator?

Or a mentor, a leader, a man of God If I had told you at the time,

Put childish words onto my experience,

Barely understood, confused and defensive;

Would you have heard?

Or would you have cast it out as youthful fantasy, teenage angst, sinful desire?

If I could tell you with 100% clarity that he groped me, would that make it easier for you?

For the protesting congregation,

Who doesn't need to be concerned with the private, emotional messages sent between a teacher and his pupil.

Would you like me to cry?

To tell you about the impact this has had; does that make it easier for you?

Does it make you uncomfortable, guilty, turning away?

Would you like me to be calm, rational, quiet?

Would that help you manage your emotions, or would you question why I'd bother,

Why drag up all this unpleasantness?

Accept it and move on.

Can I be angry?

Or is that the mark of a 'woman scorned', a lost soul, of the world, fallen far from God's embrace? Are my emotions demonic?

Is the devil working through me?

Should I have prayed more, begged for forgiveness, stayed quiet and served?

Is it all a big fuss about nothing?

How can I make this easier for you?

Easier for him?"

We are so, so much better than this!

We will delve into the theology and practices that help create these destructive, unsafe cultures later before exploring how psychological safety and courageous followership can act as remedies. But for now, it's time to tell my story. It paves the way.

DAVID WARREN

Chapter 2
My Story Of (Nearly) Everything

Our lives are shaped by many factors: education, family, friends, culture, church, economics and many others. My autonomous self likes to think I have come to my faith standpoints in such a way that I consider my way to be the 'biblical' way. I hope my tribe is more biblical than all the others. The trouble is that my theology and belief systems are not just a result of my Bible study but also products of my history. The "me" of today is a complex mix of all the "mes" of all my yesterdays.

"I met with one of the elders who was concerned I had asked Sarah to be our guest preacher at the church. I was told that they had never had a lady preacher. I wondered why and was told they never had a lady preacher because it was unbiblical. I dug a bit and it was obvious he couldn't coherently argue his standpoint from the Bible other than basic text quoting from the usual Pauline passages. The truth was, his argument was based on history and tradition. It was an inadequate answer not because he was right or wrong but because he couldn't explain the standpoint from the Bible."

To understand the what and why of our thinking and actions, we must dig into our history and see it as a living story that is still creating who we are. I should be becoming a better version of myself. Is this not what the Holy Spirit does if we allow Him to?

What follows is a short history of my life and how it has interacted with God's story and the stories of others. It helps me (and I hope you) to understand why I have ended up writing a book to challenge the church to reshape her story in a more healthy, fearless and safe way. Reflecting on 47 years (it starts with me as an 18-year-old) of church leadership in one form or another, I am persuaded (I would say by the leading of the Spirit) that some of my thinking and practices over the years have been misplaced and even unsafe. I am also persuaded that the churchy world that has been such an influence on my thinking and practice also needs to reflect, learn and change. I have been a bit too much like the elder in the story above who built his belief of women in leadership on the sand of "That's the way it is" without really knowing why and never asking the tough questions.

My story is part of God's story; so, I don't look back with any sense of despair. It has been a wonderful journey and I am amazed how God has changed so many lives. The positives far outweigh any negatives. But, as I tell the teachers I now try to mentor, "The best leaders are always learning." It is far too easy to end up reflecting the views of our tribes, colleges and training courses without ever asking ourselves and those we work alongside tough questions. "That's the way it has always been" or "That's the way we do it" are never enough. Many of us aren't brave enough to ask ourselves some very tough questions about the "why" of abusive leadership cultures. The story (along with all the others I tell) helps to explain why I have come to this conclusion.

My Story

It was time to have a chat with the minister. I was a Methodist then and part of a thriving youth group. For a while I had been feeling that I was being called to be a Methodist Minister. We sat down and I will never forget John's wise words. "Don't do it until you almost physically have no choice." It struck a chord. It wasn't to be an easy ride — there would be a price to pay and there was no rush. He was a good shepherd. The next conversation was with our amazing youth leader, Roland. He and his wife, Margaret, shaped those crucial teenage years more than anyone else. As usual I couldn't get past the front door without a hug from Margaret (she said she didn't have many gifts, but we all knew she loved us dearly) and there on the coffee table was a prospectus for Cliff College. He had anticipated the conversation and had a suggestion to make. Roland was like that. He knew us. He gathered us. He loved us. He was a good shepherd. Forty years later, many of that band of young people gathered again to celebrate Roland's life which never included a stage, a sermon, worship leading or an image. He served and loved, and I have the feeling his style of leadership will become more and more important and fruitful.

The late 70s and early 80s were exciting times for many in the church and deeply worrying for others. The charismatic renewal, the house church movement and a growing Pentecostal influence were shaping the future, but for some this was all very threatening. How on earth does that overhead projector in front of the flowers help us worship, let alone that guitar! Roland had gently introduced us to this new world. Little did I know then how deeply involved I would become. My world was the Methodist world plus a few visits to celebrations that lifted the soul and excited this young and easily influenced teenager. I had no idea that the seeds of this book were being sown in those early, exciting and very naive days.

I am reminded of meeting and listening to Gerald Coates who was a rising star of the time and a highly regarded (if a little controversial) leader. He was inspiring and the church was dynamic and growing. It was one of many what became called "apostolic hubs" emerging around the nation. Years later a report investigating allegations against Mr Coates[1] joined other such reports revealing unprofessional, harmful and unwise ministry practices dating back over many years. Looking back, I am now convinced that there remain many untold stories that darken the undoubted growth and fruitfulness of those exciting days. At the time, there were numerous rumours, stories and denials of "heavy shepherding" (perhaps we would call it spiritual abuse today) and the press were all over some of the more well-known house churches.

The desire to restore the church to New Testament patterns of leadership and ministry were understandable and exciting but it also provided healthy soil from which abuse could grow. It is interesting that names from the established churches around that time also hit the news headlines, e.g. Jonathan Fletcher and John Smyth. At the time of writing, consequences are still being worked through and many victims await proper apologies and meaningful accountability. Many victims continue to suffer. The years of my youth and early twenties were exciting and the new movements, styles and methodologies made my Methodist Church look a tad traditional and lacking vitality. As another leader in those days, Bryn Jones would preach, "Time to come out from amongst them."

Now married and qualified as a Religious Education and Geography teacher, it was time to move to Kent. Borden Grammar School for boys awaited my lack of teaching skills in the secondary school setting. Jayne (we met at Cliff Marriage College!) and I hoped the local Methodist minister would welcome us into their fold, but she had other ideas, and it was clear very early on that having a young, enthusiastic, charismatic couple in their midst would mean trouble. She was probably right! By then suspicion of the "new" was deeply embedded in some circles. We joined a brand-new church plant with a group of churches called New Frontiers. We loved the folks and the vision, even though I was a big pain to Barry and Maureen Gould who faithfully led the church. Despite my unhelpfulness, Barry and Maureen kept in touch from time to time which has been a delight. New Frontiers was, for me, a whole new way of doing church and the message of grace taught so clearly by Terry Virgo had a huge impact. I am not quite so convinced of some aspects of reformed theology nowadays, but I hold these days dear in my heart. They were foundational in so many ways. We attended the final Downs Bible week and began the exciting journey of the Stoneleigh Bible Week, leadership training and finally a request to lead a church in Cranbrook. They were good years, and we learnt much. Our children were inspired by all that Stoneleigh offered and we don't regret a single moment. Unknown to me at the time, more seeds for this book were being sown as speakers such as C.J. Mahaney and the Kansas City Prophets had their influence in conferences and gatherings. These men were key speakers, and their books were recommended. They were held up as examples of great leadership and ministry but have since disappointingly joined the ever-growing list of scandalised and abusive leadership in one form or another. Some stories dating back to the Stoneleigh era remained hidden for many years and the consequences are still very real and painful for many. This is a summary of one such story:

"As a teenager I was physically abused by a church leader. The elders failed to act other than to cast out the demons they were convinced this leader had. No other action was taken. I have since told my story in court and others have told theirs. The leader was found guilty. I then went through the struggle of knowing the leaders who knew would never apologise. The church took many months before finally releasing an apology. The leaders who knew remain silent."

This kind of story is far too common. Some make the excuse that "this was the way things were done then". Whatever the truth or otherwise of this overused argument, we create more "others" by refusing to accept responsibility and finding excuses as to why we can't apologise when finally the light shines on those dark corners. Sincere and meaningful apology can be hard to give, but sadly it is often harder to find. More about forgiveness later.

I do remember the Kansas City Prophets being quite the thing back then. Here were men predicting amazing events with the ability to "see" into all kinds of situations as well as into the future. It was astounding to read and hear the stories. In recent months another of that particular gang, Mike Bickle, has been added to the list of influential leaders who have been revealed to be manipulative and abusive. One of the questions that must continue to be asked and must bug us all until we find better answers is, "How on earth did we not notice something was so, so wrong?" and "What systems do we create that so easily hide appalling behaviours over many years?"

Cranbrook was a mix of huge fun with some wonderful young families and massive struggles with a whole variety of difficult pastoral and leadership issues cropping up. By now, in my early 30s, I was hardly equipped to deal with the most challenging of pastoral situations. I was delighted to have the active and practical support of the growing New Frontiers family. I remain unsure about some aspects of the who, what and how of apostles and prophets, but I do know that where relationships, gifts and perspectives come together, we can create supportive, healthy and constructive cultures. Leaders should never stand alone and relationships are key to survival when mistreated (more about this later).

A mentor friend once suggested to me that perhaps tough seasons are all part of the "sufferings of Christ". We remember our time in Cranbrook with great fondness. Our kids grew up happily and we had so much fun with Kids Clubs, Stoneleigh Bible Week and so much more. Whilst the joys outweighed the challenges, it was clear that the underlying foundations of the church were too weak and too mixed up to build on, so we all agreed a fresh start was needed. It became clear that it would be far better for the church to be part of Kings Church, Hastings and for Jayne and I to move to the Midlands to be part of what New Frontiers called the "Midlands Initiative". Many years later, the pastor of the Vine Church (which was planted later into Cranbrook) contacted me to apologise on behalf of some of the Cranbrook folks as to how they said their "goodbyes" to us. They had an offering and presented Jayne and

I with a cheque for £1000. The church can be a place of amazing grace, forgiveness and kindness. It meant so much. These are the kind of actions that help create healthy cultures.

Our next stop was Nuneaton. We were excited to be asked to lead a church linked to New Frontiers. Sadly this all fell apart very soon after we arrived. It was painful for everyone involved. The apostle at the time offered us a one hour meeting after a church service six weeks ahead. What seems like Godly busyness can become the root of harm and a lack of care. We were deeply impacted by the lack of care and understanding shown and this part of our adventure journey cost us significant sums of money and much sadness. Promises were openly and publicly broken and apostolic leaders failed to take any responsibility for decisions they made.

Fortunately, I had a great job in a local primary school and the leaders of the nearby Assembly of God church were amazing and quickly responded with a meal invite a week after my initial call. The contrast was huge. We loved being part of what was then called Bedworth Christian Centre. The kids missions teams were crazy fun and to help develop a leadership training centre was rewarding.

Out of the blue, the senior pastor called and asked me to preach at a struggling church in Hinckley. This was the start of a very happy nine years growing and developing a thriving church. The Hinckley folks were amazing and so generous. Difficult decisions had to be made but the willingness to move forward and leave a sad season behind was commendable and not easy for some. Step by step, we developed a pre-school, cheered on Rocky Kids, tried to enthuse Fusion Youth, helped develop effective family support work in primary schools and supported the development of a new mental health charity called "Accept". When it was time to begin the process to move on, the foundations of a wonderful new community centre were being laid. Exciting times.

During these Hinckley years I had the privilege to travel to Romania on numerous occasions. Many teams followed from different churches. I lost count of the number of times I've jumped on board the Bucharest flight and at the time of writing this sentence, I am settling back home after yet another trip to see close friends and the wonderful folks at Speranta Church, Galati. I am so proud of the wonderful success stories some of the young folks we worked with in Calarasi now tell. As we tell the dark stories, we must never forget the numerous and powerful stories of lives changed and communities impacted with the amazing "Good News of the Kingdom". More about Romania later!

I was also privileged to teach the Network Course (out of Willow Creek) in numerous churches. Bill Hybells, the leader of Willow Creek, was considered to be one of the great leadership gurus and our parent church in Bedworth enjoyed visits from Brian Houston (Hillsong) and many other internationally known speakers. We also sent many youth to the emerging Soul Survivor camps under the leadership of Mike Pilavachi.

I could never have imagined that many of the leaders in that season whom I admired and learnt so much from wouldn't make it to the end without scandal of one form or another. More seeds had been sown and more stories emerged. The explanation often given is that these (mainly men) leaders are just like you and me and "there by the grace of God go I". There is truth in this but we can't allow simplistic sayings to excuse appalling practices and to explain why leaders and organisational processes help create the cultures that seem to emerge in far too many settings. Below the surface lie power, pride, greed and performance that combine to create fear, and where fear reigns, so will sin.

I have never been frightened of a challenge. I love turning things around or creating new ways of serving the community through the church. Someone once said, "The trouble with David is that if he hasn't got anything to fix, he will create something to be fixed." Our greatest strengths can also be the place where danger lurks. And so to our next adventure. The beautiful nation of New Zealand awaited our arrival! It was time to create further impetus for the work of Next Level International in eastern Europe. All the work had been done, promises made and contacts established. Little did I know that this particular adventure would be the catalyst to so much re-thinking of so many things.

Before we tell stories from this season, it is important to stress that most leaders I have come across have been amazing: faithful, kind, supportive and very Jesus-focused. This was as true in New Zealand as it had always been in the United Kingdom. I am not out to criticise for the sake of it, but to share what I and others experienced so we can all learn how we can do things better. To hide our heads in the sand and pretend there aren't very real problems is foolish and can only mean more pain is inflicted. Light needs to shine in the dark places that are pretending to be light.

Big churches and their leaders are often placed on the big platforms. Success is measured by numbers. If the image looks good, the performance sounds good and the numbers are good, then surely all is good! It was a privilege to be a part of Harbourside Church (now KingdomCity) for a year. The Christmas show, the annual conference and Martin Steel's series on the End Times were highlights. These guys did things well and most folks seemed very happy as they attended the services and went to various groups. But underneath all the show I began to discover that all was not as it seemed. The back door was nearly as big as the front and there were stories being told of unhealthy pastoral practices, theology and leadership. As leaders, we are all too easily fooled by the show and end up acting, assuming the ends justify the means and then persuade ourselves that the moaners are troublemakers and hence are wise to move on. It is them; not us. On reflection, I have often done just that. I am sorry.

My aim is not to have a go at Harbourside Church, but the stories told have been hidden for too long and too many people suffered. I only tell a few of the many here to illustrate and I commend the bravery of those who now speak out. Names, times and dates are altered or missed out whilst job titles and roles are fictional. I also share one of my own stories from this season. It's sad to say that such stories have been told from many other settings (I have read the official reports and stories and spoken to people from churches and Christian ministry settings in the UK, Australia, USA and New Zealand). It took 12 years to make part of the story public on Facebook. Sadly and surprisingly, many others responded with their stories. It is tragic, but until light is shone into these dark places, my churchy world will never learn. We are better than this!

"I (David) sat in a staff and internship meeting being led by a senior leader (I wasn't technically a member of staff but was invited). During his little message, this bigger than life, authority figure shared how fed up and disturbed he was with criticism. It was unhelpful and unbiblical. Criticism was a sign of rebellion. We must resist the spirit of criticism. We were then asked to go into the auditorium, walk around the building and speak against this critical spirit. It was disturbing nonsense. I just couldn't do what I was being asked so went to my office and wrote an email to express my concern about the meeting. I was summoned to meet three of the senior leaders (I was on my own) who proceeded to tell me that I was mistaken and that this was all about my disappointment that

European contacts had not gone as well as I had hoped. It was my fault. The email was then torn up by that powerful leader and thrown across the floor. I left, astonished at the manipulation and incompetence of it all. That same leader later swore and shouted at me when I thanked him for leading another meeting well. I was 'unimportant' and 'useless' and should not talk to him again. What was even more disturbing was how the two other leaders in the room simply accepted the word of their fellow leader without question. They were not at that infamous meeting."

What are people supposed to do? I am a fighter (a strength which has sometimes got me into trouble) so I decided to seek the advice of the "apostolic advisers" mentioned on the website. Surprise, surprise — the two available to talk to were both being given money to support their ministry. I tried but nothing happened. "That's just the way he is" was the response. This phrase emerges as a common and dangerous excuse used in many abusive settings.

"As a young, brainless male, part of me wanted to believe that this senior leader's swearing, name calling, strategic manipulation, and 'straight talking' was merely a kind of cool, edgy, militant version of Christianity, that I never knew was acceptable. While I tried my best to dismiss it, I always had a nagging sense of unease. As I matured and shared my experiences with more experienced and wiser Christians, I quickly came to understand that this leader had absolutely no business working for a Christian organisation that ostensibly existed to represent Christ to the world, and disciple and care for people."

And...

"When I raised concerns about the behaviour of a male pastor, I was told I was being disrespectful of a man of God and I was misinterpreting his actions. He was later convicted for procuring an underaged girl for sex."

And...

"In my time on staff, I went from young, committed, optimistic and certain that I was on God's path for my life to being confused and seeing a psychologist and suffering physically, mentally and spiritually. Burn out, breakdown, anxiety, panic attacks and depression were part of my life for a season. I tried to share with the leadership how I was struggling. I was told that it was part of my training and the analogy of a coach who pushes his athletes to the point of vomiting or passing out, so as to increase their physical capacity was used. My psychologist at the time said this was complete nonsense and had no place in Christlike formation."

And...

"You could never disagree with him, because he would just overpower you. He used awful language, would degrade people in public, make nasty comments about people in the congregation in staff meetings, and made me feel like I was treading on eggshells every day."

Looking back, I have no hesitation in saying this was a toxic and abusive culture. It was a deeply unsafe space for many and as a result, family and friends were hurt and still speak of their pain. Trauma doesn't just go away over time. Nothing was done and many people were ignored or told to go away in no uncertain terms. To this day, leaders involved knew about the abusive behaviours and remain convinced that the bullying, manipulation and tantrums were all just misunderstandings of a style of leadership. Lame excuses for silence have been far too common in various settings where abusive leadership has been revealed to be what it really is.

It was a wonderful year in so many ways. I ran many kilometres a week and we loved the coffee culture, beaches and wonderful scenery. We met amazing people and remain thankful that a few contacts made were a help in the big picture plan in eastern Europe. In many ways it was tough and money was very short. We watched and listened to many stories of what I now understand as spiritual abuse. I was also unable to function as national leader of the charity, as the trustees were unable (unwilling) to meet as a group. I was told by the church leadership that the chair of trustees (the senior pastor of Harbourside) was either on Sabbatical, was too busy and once that I "wasn't important enough". In the end, we were rescued by Ps Ken Harrison (then the leader of the Assembly of God in New Zealand) who held the Next Level International (New Zealand) leaders accountable and subsequently the New Zealand branch closed down. Ps Ken and many others continue to serve the churches in eastern Europe to this day and I have had the joy of working with Ken in a number of Romanian settings. Jayne and I remain thankful to Ken and Raewyn for their love, generosity and friendship. Even in the most difficult ministry seasons, we discover gold in many people.

"Jayne and I were flying home in two days. Our landlady had refused to refund our house deposit and we were left with just a few dollars and no cash for when we returned home. Ken and Raewyn were taking us out for a farewell lunch. On the way, he suddenly stopped the car and went to a cash machine. 'God just told me to give you this' and he handed over a significant sum of money. He knew nothing of our circumstances. Two days later, on our way to the airport we were able to go to the bank and take out the deposit money which had been withheld for no good reason. The estate agent was furious with his client — as were we. We were able to return home with enough to keep us going until work kicked in."

We landed back in the UK with £500 in the bank and I headed into a new life and challenge as senior leader of St Paul's Church, Worcester. Jayne was quickly re-employed as a Family Support worker, so all was quickly sorted. For the next five years I felt a bit like Nehemiah. Clearing rubble, building new walls and resisting being sidetracked. It was fun, challenging, happy and really creative!

We made great friends and had the privilege of serving some of the most creative and inspirational leaders I've ever met. The transformation was remarkable and can only be put down to the grace of God and the hard work of key people. I will never forget the first elders' meeting. A huge gas bill could not be paid, the electrical system was below standard, meaning insurances were invalid, there were serious safeguarding issues, stories to be told and a financial situation far worse than I had been told. Big decisions had to be made extremely quickly and were often interpreted as harsh and uncaring. I knew what the bigger pictures were. Safeguarding standards, health and safety issues and the law of the land must be followed. Some would have felt I was the saviour of a failing and dysfunctional church whilst others thought I was the devil in disguise. On reflection, I was probably too strong at times and perhaps rude and overbearing at times. I am sorry. I honestly acted to protect vulnerable people, develop safe employment and volunteering practices whilst also trying to solve some very deep issues.

"John and a small group of friends served the homeless each week by handing out simple food packages and providing a signposting service to help where they could. I had a deep respect for the work. Unfortunately the church was not adequately insured and it was unclear whether we or another organisation was responsible. I decided for the safety and security of these folks that we had to be really clear as to who was responsible, so insurance and the like were clear. The other organisation was far better placed at the time to take it on board and we would simply provide kitchen facilities for free. All was good. A little while later, a video appeared on

YouTube accusing me of racial discrimination and doing the work of the devil by stopping a vital service to the poor because they were in danger of being stabbed."

Tough decisions can be misinterpreted. To one, a tough decision is wise leadership; to another, that same decision is the work of the devil!

A Jesus-centred community must be a serving community. We serve not to find clever ways of getting as many people from hell to heaven. We must be careful of motive as people need to trust us before they hear us. CityCare aimed to "pastor the city" without any motive other than serving. Over the years, hundreds (probably thousands) were supported through education and health projects, care for the elderly and family, support for youth, families and children. They were exciting days. Finances were sorted and the large Grade 2 listed building vastly improved. It really was a miracle. On the journey it was wonderful that some discovered they were loved by Christ. Dot Burnett walked this whole journey with great faithfulness, creativity and honesty. She is now the wonderful senior leader of St Paul's. I am delighted she has made many more changes and has developed a whole new team. Church life is never static and change is always on the agenda. Many more have now found Jesus really is alive and well.

During this time the trustees allowed me to complete an MA in Missional Leadership. This began to open my eyes to some new thinking around followership and (a little later) psychological safety. New sad stories concerning the likes of Bill Hybells, Ravi Zacherias, Mark Driscoll and others also began to emerge. More seeds were being sown as to how we develop safe, healthy cultures where leaders can lead well and people can "follow" well (much more will follow in the Interludes). More and more stories were being told of abusive leadership in various settings.

"The phone rang. During a conversation a young person had told the caller that they had been sexually abused by a church leader a few years prior. The senior leader was informed of the complaint. The allegation was not pursued and no proper report was made as the accused pleaded innocent and was believed. Nothing was done. Abuse can live with people for many years before courage is found to tell the story. In this case, the accuser did everything right from day one and her courage was squashed by leaders who believed the man in authority rather than the girl who lacked influence to do any more for many years."

These kinds of stories are far too common for any church leader to think that all is well within our systems and leadership. I have been shocked that even in my small world with little influence so many have written or told me their story of appalling treatment at the hands of church leaders and institutions.

Our time at St Paul's was up. I simply didn't sense any mandate from God to go beyond the five years agreed. It was a tough decision and many were shocked and surprised (some delighted). I have learnt that it is never wise for a church leader to continue when there is no mandate; no new sense of vision and direction. Church leadership is a calling; not a career. A new and very different role then emerged and we settled into the All Nations family in Wolverhampton. I hoped this would provide a home and base where I could use the skills, knowledge and experiences gained over the years to support and develop what seemed to be an exciting and emerging new movement.

I walked into a very different culture with very different values and leadership perspectives. It was tough and looking back, it was an unhealthy place for me to be (that is extremely difficult to write). Ps Steve Uppal and the team were amazing people in so many ways. An unmatched commitment to prayer and a passion for revival drove the church and All Nations movement forward, but I found myself more and more uncomfortable with some aspects of leadership, theology and practice. More prayer, more Scripture reading, more fasting, more discipline. Sometimes values can become unwritten laws or standards to attain rather than for what they were intended. The seeds sown over the years were beginning to emerge as they grew roots and shoots. Eventually I resigned (badly). At the time, I felt I had little choice as my mental and spiritual health were suffering. It was super tough as Steve had given me the opportunity to oversee a number of congregations which I thoroughly enjoyed and through which we made good friends. Underneath it all, however, I felt I was being asked or sometimes told to be someone I really wasn't. I wasn't able to be the best me and this was psychologically unsafe. I was beginning to understand the dynamics of spiritual stress in the church in a deeper and more personal way. I started the journey of serious reflection and rethinking of many aspects of the Christian world I had been a part of for so many years.

After All Nations, I took up a pastoral role in Loughborough which was financially scuppered by Covid, and so the only option was to pass the church to a larger Assemblies of God church in the town. A move to Lincoln followed. I won't dwell on this short period other than to say sometimes it is a challenge to understand the "why" question in the Christian life. I have a feeling we were placed in Loughborough simply to keep the wonderful folks at Beacon Church together over Covid. I do reflect that many had been excited by numerous 2020 prophecies before Covid hit. The Covid season was littered with the so-called prophets predicting revival was just around the corner. One leader whom I knew well declared that God had told him none of his congregation would die. It all added to my growing unease. The theology interlude below will add some further thoughts on all this.

Chapter 3
The Romanian Story

I didn't want to go to Romania but my children persuaded me. We all headed out to Calarasi where we worked alongside Bethany House and met Ps Iulian for the first time. The girls in the house had their sad stories to tell — abuse, neglect and fear. Dan and Daniela did an awesome job as they sought to love, care and develop these precious young lives in the most difficult of environments.

It was the last day of our first visit to Romania. It had been a tough week for some, but all were delighted to have made the trip. Some team members were overwhelmed with what they saw and heard, but we were better people for the experience.

"I (David) sat opposite Emanuela at the meal table. She was a feisty young girl who clearly had the potential to go far in life! Sharp, intelligent and not afraid to argue. Towards the end of the meal, I tried to encourage Emanuela by saying we would see her again. Her reply shocked and inspired me. 'No, you won't. Everyone says that!' she exclaimed clearly and with passion. Her experience told her that teams from here and there would come, make promises and never return. She was feeling very let down. I promised her I would be the exception to the rule. I went back to Bethany House at least twice a year every year until those wonderful young girls became young ladies and a new cohort arrived on the scene. I believe Emanuela now lives in South America and is married to a pastor and a mum to her own kids."

All the leadership books, conferences and comforts of home church felt a million miles away in those early days. Leadership meant suffering, long hours, no pay, reliance on support from folks like us and poverty. Pastors had often been persecuted, spies placed in their churches and rumours were deliberately spread. It is no wonder it has taken a generation to begin to build trust within the church. Many of the more difficult conversations were a direct result of this culture of suspicion and mistrust. Given all that had happened, this was unsurprising.

After refusing to allow us to install central heating in his small, overcrowded and extremely cold apartment we managed to persuade Ps Iulian to have a heater installed in his kitchen. His conviction was that none of his people had much heating, so why should he? He remains a hero. Over the years I had the joy of dedicating children, marrying a couple and speaking at numerous churches in and around Calarasi, Constanta and Galati. Many of those young girls are now adults with children and great jobs in different nations. One is a doctor in Germany, another a pastor in Brazil with two wonderful kids, another a real estate manager with three lovely children, another a wonderful mum in Italy and another stayed in Romania and has a wonderful family (I do not know all their stories and where they all are now).

Jesus changes lives and even as we discuss abusive leadership and church cultures we must never forget that God's grace really does work. The overwhelming majority of my experiences have been positive and healthy and the stories that can be told are amazing. One such story is that of Ps Nelu in Galati. He is another one of my heroes. In 2004 he started to dream of a new church that was to be radically different from the very traditional Romanian Pentecostal Church he was leading. He was one of the pastors supported by Next Level International. Over the years, we have developed a great friendship. He has never asked for money and has always kept his word and acted with integrity when others in similar situations were finding more "creative" ways to live and lead! Ps Nelu is a great example that it is possible to walk through the toughest ministry life with a whole heart.

In this book, you will read many sad stories where the church really does need to do better. In the midst of it all, amazing people serve, suffer and sacrifice. As I look back over the years, it is these people that shine light into the dark spaces. These are the heroes of faith. We live in a day where we think the story is being told by the stars of the platform and conference circuit, by hits on YouTube and clever stories on Instagram. I have a feeling God looks at it all and knows His story is actually being told far away from the stage and lights. Iulian, Nelu, Traian, Eleana, Adi et al. are the writers, actors and light bearers.

"We gathered in the courtyard of a small two-room house. Mum, dad and a few kids (not sure how many) lived there. There was a fire pit dug into the mud in the corner of the little plot. Each day, the dad would travel on his cart and collect old metal and create new cooking pots in the pit. A pot a day to sell was a good outcome for the labour. We listened to their story and he asked if we would like to sing. Out came the piano accordion and the father (also a pastor) started to play and sing. His face shone. The joy was palpable. Tears flowed. At the end of our time, we were presented with a large silver pot. We couldn't refuse to take it even though we knew it represented a day's salary. On return to the UK we auctioned that pot to help pay for various support in Romania and a young lady who was on the team bought it for a significant sum of money which was used to support the work of Bethany House."

The generosity and faith of a father and pastor in a village with a handful of Christians shone far wider than he could ever have imagined. I have a feeling this is more like an Acts church than much of what we see and experience in the western world today. Dare I say it? This pastor reflected more characteristics of a true apostle than many who claim to be apostles today: whoops, I said it!

Sometimes a large percentage of Christians forget where the reality of the Christian life is worked out. According to a 2010 report, only about 25% of Christians in the world live in Europe. 25% live in sub-Saharan Africa. 13% in Asia and the Pacific.[2] Millions live in poverty and struggle to make ends meet. Many are persecuted. Their stories are easily forgotten in the midst of a Christian world caught up in fame, power and control rather than the good news of a new creation where justice (putting right what is so broken) flows.

There were, of course, Romanian stories of poor and abusive leadership, financial mismanagement and just plain craziness. Many painful stories were written in the context of ignorance as the Christian community often drew water from the deep well of mistrust dug by the history of the nation. We are foolish to ignore history as its impact goes deeper and its reach wider than we'd like to think.

DAVID WARREN

Chapter 4
Sophie's Story

The young lady who writes is brave, honest and brilliant at her work and one more heroine who has told her story. I know it to be true! Sadly some of the leaders involved remain ignorant of their ignorance and unaware of the pain they have caused. I suspect some will still feel their theology and practice were Biblical and justified. It was Sophie's fault! There are many more stories like this yet to be told and many more I am unable to write about. I really do hope that the "shepherds" and the institution involved will one day accept responsibility and find it in their hearts to apologise and make rightful recompense. I sadly doubt that will happen. As we have been telling the stories you may well notice that themes are beginning to emerge. We will look into these in more detail in the Theology Interlude. It isn't an easy chapter to write.

"I was a teenager when I found my way into the Pentecostal Church movement in Auckland, New Zealand. Life had been turned on its head and I was confused, hurting and most of all vulnerable. I was told that the church would offer me a place of solace, support and friendship. Things started well. The Gospel of grace and the absolute love of Jesus Christ was preached from the platform. People were kind, caring and inclusive. I felt sure they'd accept me as me.

'Come to Jesus, as you are,' they'd say. 'Jesus loves and accepts everyone, exactly as they are.' That was all fine until you didn't conform to the standards set as sufficient for a member of their congregation.

It was a baptism of fire. I first attended church in April, I was 'saved' in May and by November I was a member of the church's staff. A 'baby Christian' in my journey, I was so unsure of what I had walked into. I was desperate to be accepted and was thrust headfirst into the chaos and toxic culture that I have discovered to be rife in so many Pentecostal churches.

I never imagined that what I experienced inside the church would traumatise me more than anything I experienced outside of the church. By the time I left, I was a shell of my former self. I'd forgotten what it felt like to feel like a whole, healthy person. It took years of therapy, reflection and searching to rediscover who I believed I was fundamentally made to be, whether that's by the God they preached about or some other higher power — I'm still undecided. But what I do know is, they certainly weren't acting in the way that reflected what they preached. It was hypocrisy. My stories and traumatic experiences I faced and ultimately why I chose to leave are told below. The reality is I found more love, care and support outside of the church than I ever did inside of it.

Not long after I decided to follow Christ, I discovered that I had been sexually abused as a child and in an attempt to protect me my family had kept it from me.

I had flashback memories that came in waves and parts came back to me at the most inconvenient times. It ultimately answered so many questions I'd had about my issues, fears and inability to be intimate with a partner. Suddenly it all made sense. I spoke to my pastors about this and remember responding to an altar call specifically relating to childhood abuse. The pastor who prayed for me, told me I needed to ask God for forgiveness (I needed to ask forgiveness for being sexually abused as a child! This now sounds unbelievable.). I was told that I needed to break the soul tie that had connected me to this pedophile for the rest of my life. That I needed to be 're-virginised'. I was made to feel dirty and like somehow what had happened to me was my fault. I was told not to disclose this information to future partners as it would likely make them feel like I hadn't saved myself for them.

My boss at the time was a bully. He used intimidation tactics to scare me, and the other younger staff, into submission. The young men on the team were called 'poofters' and told they were 'too soft'. When any of us tried to implement any kind of work/life balance of working relationship boundaries around not being contacted outside of hours or not working overtime for free, we were told that we 'didn't believe in advancing the kingdom', we were 'doing God's work' and that 'God didn't have timelines or hours'. Ultimately, some of us were working 60, 70 sometimes 80-hour weeks and paid for 40 hours or less. I was paid for 32 hours per week. When we were tired, or we mentioned feeling burned out, we were told that the only reason we were burnt out was because we were 'working from our own tank and not from God's tank' and basically if we read our Bible more and prayed more, we wouldn't be so tired.

Every Tuesday morning, we had a staff prayer meeting. One particular week my boss, who was leading the session, wanted to 'pray life into the 9 am service' — the 9 am service was predominantly older people and young families who worship/encounter God in a quiet more reflective kind of way. It just didn't sit with me and the clear implication was that they weren't as 'passionate' as they should be. I disagreed and politely declined to pray in this way. I believed that praying for something I fundamentally didn't believe in was wrong. What happened next was beyond comprehension. I was labeled 'insubordinate' and was pulled into numerous disciplinary meetings and was told that I needed to attend counseling sessions if I wanted to keep my job. These sessions were with a church-appointed counselor and can only be described as modern-day exorcism. I was intimidated and terrified of losing my job and so, as I'm sure they knew I would, I complied. And of course, my progress was reported back.

I'm a quirky, fun-loving, extroverted personality. I can be outspoken; I fight for the underdog and stand up for what I believe in. I fight for what I think is right, and injustice makes me furious. All these things can make me fiery and passionate. In hindsight these qualities were all things the pastors disliked about me. The traits were all a part of my 'rebellious spirit' and were things that I needed cast out of me, to be who they told me God wanted me to be. They were determined to shut me down, minimise my spirit and ultimately make me the 'cookie cutter' Christian that would be easy to manage and control so they could advance their agenda.

On recommendation from one of the pastors, I found an external counselor who didn't have room to take on more clients. So, she recommended her daughter, who was also a qualified psychotherapist. This woman would go on to be one of the few people I trusted implicitly with my deepest, darkest, craziest thoughts. She encouraged me to explore all aspects of myself, and together we weeded and deconstructed what I'd learned and been told about myself and rediscovered the 'real me'. Seeing her over the years enabled me to maintain my sanity. At times, when things got really bad in church, my bosses, under the guise of wanting to 'support me' requested multiple times to talk to her. They attempted to bully me into giving them permission to discuss the intimate details of our sessions despite, at times, me feeling that I had no choice but to comply. She never disclosed any information about me, she wasn't afraid to tell them she thought it was inappropriate and she continued to encourage me to stand up for myself. I continued to see her for more than 15 years and together we unpacked the religious trauma. She helped me heal. Of course, there are always things we can work on, develop and grow, but overall, I am proud of the woman I have become. I owe a huge amount of that to her patience, encouragement and guidance.

Despite them trying to mold me into what they wanted, ultimately, I wouldn't comply. There were parts of me they just couldn't crush, and I think I became, in their eyes, a liability. So when all else failed it was time for me to go. As quickly as they swept me up into their world, I was discarded. I was made redundant from my role at church and my life came crashing down around me. Despite my experiences, and the hurt, it had become all I knew and to lose it all, in one foul swoop felt like more than I could bear.

Once I was made redundant and no longer on staff, I attempted to remain a part of the community. Over the course of three years the church had managed to become my entire life. I had very few friends outside of church, and I had become distant from my family. To leave all together would mean leaving my life behind. That, and I didn't even know who I was anymore. After all, my personality was a 'demon'. And all the things that make me "me" I'd been told were bad.

As I moved through therapy, and landed my first corporate job and made some new friends, I slowly came to understand that I was a good person and that people wanted to be my friend — the real me, not the fake me. I was capable of so much more. I realised the world outside of the church was big and bright and was offering me so much more than the world inside.

Since then, I have watched a number of people I went to church with, also be chewed up and spat out by the same system that left me discarded and broken. I have picked myself back up, with the help of some incredible professionals, and amazing friends. I have built a life I am loving living and a career in corporate that I am so proud of. It hurt, and it had a profound impact on me at the time, but it's part of my journey. Every piece of what I have been through makes me who I am. Despite everything, I still care about people, I still fight for the underdog, and I still want to believe the best in everyone. I personally have chosen to 'stick it' to the entire church establishment by living a full and passionate life."

Let this story speak for itself.

DAVID WARREN

Chapter 5
The Story Through Leadership Eyes

The last thing I ever wanted to do when I accidentally set out on the new journey of discovery with regard to abusive leadership cultures was to be labelled as anti-leadership or a bitter and disappointed leader. I am pro leadership and pro church. The vast majority of leaders I have worked alongside or had the joy of meeting are amazing servants of Jesus. Leadership is tough and I think it's important to express some of the leadership struggles that play into the themes of this book.

This is not an attempt to defend myself, other leaders or the church. Some things are indefensible. But this is about building a picture of abusive cultures that need to be addressed and healed if we are to create safe cultures. The responsibility does not just lie with leaders but all of us. Psychological safety and courageous followership will illustrate the dynamics required.

We can be better than this!

"I had spent many hours working to try and help a young couple work through serious financial and marriage issues. It was impacting both families and all were in my little church. I did my best, travelling from one to another and it seemed to me all had gone as well as I could have hoped. There was peace. A few weeks later, I was asked to sit in front of the whole church and listen to everyone's view about my leadership and especially my pastoral skills. It was hard. All was going quite well until one of those whom I had thought I had helped spoke out. I was clearly uncaring, unsupportive and useless. At the end of the meeting, I was asked to comment. Everything in me wanted revenge, but I knew silence was the best course of action. Who was I to reveal the secrets of another in front of all? I was clearly going to have to take the blame."

Sometimes good shepherds protect a diseased sheep even if it costs them. Every good shepherd knows this. It is part of the shepherding deal. When entering the pastoral world, I knew this was the case, but I had no idea how challenging it could be and how difficult people were when they so desired. It can be a troubled world where trustees and powerful families can hold sway, and many seem to know what "God" has told them. There is often very little real care of pastors, nor their families and expectations can be crazily high. A fine preacher on Sunday, a wonderful counsellor on Monday, an efficient administrator on Tuesday and a hospital chaplain on Wednesday. Thursday, Friday and Saturday might also present the opportunity to be the effective evangelist, a brilliant marriage celebrant and a funeral arranger. I loved it! Along the way we make mistakes and as a dear friend pointed out in a song he once wrote, "We are cracked pots" (Mick will love this)! Sometimes we are angry and react badly.

Sometimes we shout when we shouldn't and stay silent when we should have spoken out. I have lost my temper, walked out of meetings and spoken harshly on the phone. Amid it all, a good shepherd will hold strongly to wise confidentiality and will never expose sheep to harm where there is no need to do so. A good shepherd lays down his life for the sheep. But a good shepherd can be abused, and wolves may well attack at the most surprising time.

"I was walking along the beach relaxing between Christmas and the New Year. The phone rang and it was a surprise call from a pastor friend of mine. The trustees of his church had sacked him. There had been some challenges that were being discussed and worked through, so this sudden out-of-the-blue news was both surprising and horrifying. No legal process. No care. No proper discussion. The pain was clear and the timing so cruel. How was a middle-aged pastor supposed to find a job so soon after Christmas? The pastor concerned refused to take legal action and remained calm. He protected the key players by not telling certain stories and was able to move forward with grace. The pastor's life and security can be extremely fragile and open to abusive practices from those who hold financial power."

When I started out as a pastor, communication with my church folks was mainly a telephone landline, a weekly notice sheet, verbal notices on a Sunday and regular membership meetings (or whatever your tribe called them). With the dawning of the knowledge-based society and the emergence of social media we have developed the idea that we all have the right to know whatever we want to know. It is easier to communicate but it is also more difficult! When we live in a 'demand knowledge' culture, some want us to reveal everything whilst others feel there is no need and are happy to trust their leaders. The tension between confidentiality, pastoral care and everyone-has-a-right-to-know culture is tough to navigate. Added to the mix are privacy legislation, safeguarding guidance and a whole lot more. It is inevitable that leaders get it wrong at times. We communicate too much, and folks accuse; we communicate too little, and folks accuse. Accusations are made which can easily morph into the word 'abuse'. It is a journey most leaders have travelled.

One of the things that really frustrated me at leadership conferences (and many books) was the assumption by speakers that all churches had staff, equipment and resources to spread the load of pastoral care, worship, preaching, evangelism, kids work, youth work and community transformation. It is relatively easy to delegate if it is possible to delegate! When a church is small in number (often big in heart) the leader is usually the jack of all trades and the master of none. This can be so hard and it is again inevitable that weaknesses are revealed for what they are. The notice sheet wasn't printed well on Sunday, the design wasn't up to much and please note the spelling mistake. Complaints by a small number of people in a smaller church are not easily ignored and can become a source of anxiety and even fear.

"I began to dread Monday mornings and the brown

envelope that would likely be pressed through the letter box. Yet again, I had said something, done something (or not) on Sunday that seemingly upset some nameless someone. I knew who was sending these delightful notes (she used her name and the word 'others' regularly appeared) but there was so little I could do as her husband was the treasurer and one of the three trustees. I began to dread the next Sunday. Who would I upset this week? What word or phrase would I say that was perceived to be unwise or unsuitable? Was the church falling apart by 3 pm on a Monday afternoon? This may sound so petty, but for a young starting-out pastor it is so depressing and becomes quite abusive in tone and regularity. It is bullying wrapped up in a brown envelope. I really couldn't get it right whatever I did."

And then there is money! Yep, it had to be mentioned. We need it. The church needs it. Everyone has a view on it and it won't ever go away. I've had the joy of working with some wonderful trustees who have treated me really well and tried their very best to look after myself and my family the best they could. I am grateful. It hasn't always been easy to pay the bills and have a holiday but it has been possible for me to share concerns and to be helped where possible. Sadly this is not always the case and stories of appalling salaries, long and unhealthy hours and demanding cultures are far too common. When money becomes a source of control, anxiety, fear and abuse it is clearly unacceptable. Leaders are servants but we are not slaves. Some may say, 'resign and get out'. That is so much easier to say than for some to do for all kinds of reasons: the sense of calling, the fear of failure, the ties of friendship with congregants and what the future might hold can be powerful forces. Like many abusive dynamics, words are easier than actions.

Epilogue

We can't change the story that we've written or others have written for us. It is real and it has happened. What we can do is reflect, do what we can to restore peace (shalom) in ourselves and others, and move forward into a new story doing all we can to make the "new" as bright as we can.

As I write, The Makin report about appalling abuse, leadership cover up and mismanagement in the Church of England's evangelical world has hit the headlines and the Archbishop of Canterbury has resigned. It is a stark and horrible reminder of the dark thread that runs through my story and the stories already told. It has reinforced my conviction that too much of the church is suffering from self-inflicted sickness that is in need of effective remedy and therapy. We will never pull out all these dark threads as sin will always entangle. We can however give a few threads a big pull. The interludes will help us to identify these threads more clearly so we can pull more strongly. They will also help to develop a context in which we can begin to write a whole new story.

DAVID WARREN

Part Two:
Interludes

It is time to lay some foundations for a new story that we will write. It is not perfect nor is it complete so please don't read this thinking herein lies all the answers. You may well end up asking more questions! Questions are good.

"Faith," someone once wrote, "is applying the right contents to the right picture."

I try not to go to the doctor. It usually means something is wrong with my body or mind. When I do go, I trust the expert to make an accurate diagnosis and then prescribe the correct medical solution. Sometimes extra scans or tests may be required, but my confidence is that I am in safe, expert hands.

Sadly, some of the stories told indicate that some parts of the body of Christ are suffering from the symptoms of abuse, power, control and poor (if not dangerous) pastoral practices and leadership methodologies. The cause of the pain is often badly diagnosed and symptoms assumed to be a sign of one thing when it is likely another. The serious pain I experience in my leg is caused by a problem in my spine. Correct diagnosis is vital but what is often revealed is a story of leaders overlooking the real causes of pain and placing blame on the hurting, the weak, the devil or a plot to undermine themselves, their vision and mission. Some shepherds (spiritual doctors) have proven to be incompetent, ignorant and dangerous. In the name of faith, they've applied the wrong contents to the wrong picture!

In what follows, I prescribe three medicines to the underlying sickness identified. These will help protect the body from further infection but will certainly not guarantee health. There is no space for a full analysis of the research leading to the prognosis. My aim is to help us all begin to see the right pictures and apply the right content. If faith is about allegiance to Christ above all else (which I believe was the emphasis of the word in New Testament times), then we must identify the issues and apply Christlike solutions. My contention is that the medications suggested are Christlike and bear all the hallmarks of the "Everything" Jesus offers.

Interlude 1
Theological Wisdom

French wasn't my strength at school. I would usually sit passively and copy from my friend sitting next to me. Sadly he wasn't much better at French than me, but he looked more interested. I'd often be thinking of the rugby match to be played (and probably lost) on Saturday or the chess match to be played after school somewhere around the country (which we would almost certainly win). The "unclassified" grade was the inevitable result of laziness and disengagement.

Many years later I found myself lying on a bed with extreme chest pains. The 60 Year 6 pupils whom we were responsible for were quietly amused and a bit concerned that Mr Warren was being blue-lighted to a hospital somewhere in Normandy, France. The medics must have been speaking wonderful French but I understood very little other than the word "cardiac". I had no idea of the context so inevitably thought the worse. It later emerged that they had quickly ruled out any thought of a heart attack. If I had known a bit more French, life in that moment of pain and anxiety would have been so much better. I was back with my delightful Year 6 pupils the next day and all was well. A very strong muscle had gone into spasm after a cramped and curled up night on a ferry. Poor knowledge created a lack of wisdom and a great deal of pain.

Sometimes I wonder if we can treat theology a bit like I treated French. We leave it to the experts and see very little point in delving too deeply. Much easier to disengage. We copy from the latest podcast or YouTube star and assume they are right. If they lead a big church, they must be right; just look at all those people. We may later find that some of what we've picked up is useless, unwise, unhelpful or potentially dangerous. The trouble is that as soon as we think about God, Jesus and the Bible we are beginning to touch this thing called Theology. In one sense, all Christians (and others) are theologians and we like to think we know enough about God to handle life, ourselves and others. How we see the world and how we act are bound up in how we think theologically. Poor thinking equals poor practice and very poor diagnosis of a potentially life-threatening disease.

I am not a clever theologian like those with big libraries in their offices and a brain that can write six books all at once. I've read a bit and thought a lot. In this section I've identified a few theological themes that have been treated carelessly by many. They have been the roots of abuse and harm and you will have spotted many of the issues in the stories already told. I am not claiming to be right or wrong but am suggesting that many in my churchy world have misused what they do know and forgotten that just because they hear the word "cardiac" it doesn't mean they, or someone else, is having a heart attack. Without the right diagnosis, we hit unhealthy remedies. The little French I knew was in fact extremely unhelpful. I was just plain wrong and I was not about to die!

The Bible

The Bible is complicated, extraordinary, wise, difficult, surprising, awkward, challenging, life changing, history-making, divine, human, exciting and a whole lot more! The more you think you know about it, the more there is to learn and the more certain you become, the more mysterious some of it seems to be.

It is philosophy, history, geography, sociology, science, biography, poetry and autobiography and it has sadly been used by some as a weapon to defeat the foe, to hold on to power or to manipulate the weak. The word "biblical" can easily become the bullet fired when a point has to be made or an argument won. To those spiritually abused, a quote from the Bible may even open old wounds and add to the trauma. It was the misuse of the Bible that caused the injury in the first place and the wound went deep, so great wisdom is required when we try to use the Bible as a cure. Wise Theology uses the Bible wisely!

This is not the place to discuss issues of authority, infallibility and the like. You will have your own views and your tribe, church will certainly have theirs. We like to think we are right or have the better truth. I once placed an image of a book by Richard Rohr on my Facebook page and it wasn't long before the warnings appeared. He was described as the "arch enemy" by one reader and my soul was in danger according to another. Clearly there are those who find it tough to stand outside of their theological echo-chambers. The Bible is one big inspired story about God and how His creation has interacted with itself and with Himself and eventually how He in His wisdom set about rescuing the whole of this groaning creation from sin and decay. What a story!

"We read Scripture in order to be refreshed in our memory and understanding of the story within which we ourselves are actors, to be reminded where it has come from and where it is going to, and hence what our own part within ought to be." — N.T. Wright[3]

As we look into a few particular themes we seek to use the Bible as it was intended. Wise theology never uses Scripture as a weapon or device to beat, manipulate and control, but it seeks to invite all people into the big Bible story and help people discover what part in the story they are called to play. The nature of the story means this will take listening, learning, discussion, questions, doubt, confusion and mystery. Isn't that what the centre piece and master piece of the whole story did? Jesus opened the eyes of blind people to see history or "His story". He was the "everything" to all who were lost. I now struggle with neat theological arguments and nicely constructed systematic theologies as they have a tendency to turn a wonderful, creative, truth-filled story into a school textbook in which you find all the formulas to solve the issues of life. It doesn't work like that. Theology is not a science; it is an art.

Mental Health

Over the years, my family have spent many days in various hospitals. I am delighted that the wise surgeons, nurses and doctors have applied up-to-date techniques and medications to various broken or damaged parts of the body. Just a generation ago it would have been a far more painful and probably unsuccessful and often unhealthy experience. We are complex creatures made in the image of God — a wonderful mix of body, mind and spirit that interact and create all kinds of wonderful, painful, emotional, physical and spiritual moments. The more we learn, the more amazing it is!

We now recognise that the way we think, can impact our physical well-being, whilst physical ailments make us feel "down" and can spark depressive episodes. Chemicals are released as we experience fear or joy. 13% of the global burden of ill health may come under the heading of "mental health". Theologically wise shepherds will want to understand what makes the sheep tick before applying what may well be perceived to be expert advice and care. Unfortunately too many stories told demonstrate medieval understanding followed by medieval treatment. The panic attacks may be caused by the toxic culture in a team rather than be a sign of some kind of spiritual weakness. We blame the wrong source. The advice to pray more and read the Bible more may well create more guilt and anxiety about being loved by God rather than less.

"Our senior pastor would say at our staff meeting that if you have a healthy prayer life, you would be able to work harder and harder and never get burnout. Ironically, at the time of him saying that, our local senior pastor was on leave due to burnout!"

And...

"This was the experience I had at my church. Mental illness was treated as a character or spiritual issue, and I believed it. I genuinely thought I was broken and needed fixing, but I had no idea how to do that. Pray more, read the Bible more, declare more scriptures, cast out demons. But no acknowledgement that it could just be an illness that needed treatment and support."

As there are no simple fixes to fix a broken heart or a broken back, there are no quick fixes to fix a broken soul (psyche). This is not to say that God does not or cannot heal instantaneously, but the desire to experience more of the miraculous must not hinder wise theological pastoral care. Sheep are quite right to expect their shepherds to understand their condition. So here is a Christ-centred framework into which a wise theology of mental health can be placed to help us avoid abusive practices.[4]

"I urge you, brothers and sisters (everyone), warn those who are idle and disruptive, encourage the disheartened, help the weak, be patient with everyone" (1 Thessalonians 5:14).

Admonish: Sometimes we all need those candid conversations (more about those in Interlude 3) about this or that. Poor decisions, behaviours and habits can create mental health issues.

Encourage: We can all become disheartened and anxious and sometimes this impacts our sense of balance and mood. Empathetic listening and gentle use of Scripture and prayer are healing. Some form of medical intervention may well be helpful.

Help (support): Sometimes we find it impossible to act even if we know we should. The brain may have suffered from some form of deficit or neurobiological change. We are unable to care for ourselves in the way we should. Jesus empathises with the weak (Hebrews 4:15). Specialist help and advice is a must. Most folks are not expert enough to know what to do with a broken arm; let alone a broken soul.

Patience: It takes patience from all of us. Oh, the need for pastoral patience and wisdom in so many of the stories!

Male and Female

We are living in days when gender issues are at the forefront in various settings. The debate between different sections of the church rages on and it has become a source of much anxiety, anger and abuse. We are, of course, right and it is all the others who have belief systems that create toxic and abusive cultures. It is not for this book to challenge any particular perspective but to suggest that every church structure (whether inclusive, complementarian or egalitarian or...) is vulnerable to creating unhealthy cultures.

Every church is a group of people and where there are people, there is potential for all kinds of behaviours. Your theological standpoint does however have an impact on the structures of power that might influence decision-making. Is it really healthy for power decisions that must be made as a result of male abuse of a female to be taken solely by male leaders? On one church group website I recently visited, the whole first bar of the 35 faces were male and the female was a children's worker. This shouts something to all women who have been abused or feel vulnerable.

A cursory safeguarding role for a woman (however important that role) doesn't even begin to cover the issue. An egalitarian theology doesn't solve the issue. A happy and beautiful married couple as joint "senior pastors" may create even more abusive cultures. The issue of male and female is the value of every image-bearing person and where appropriate power lies when required. Male and female must be free from fear and able to live, love and thrive in their setting (church, family or work). It is not for me to say that every woman in a complementarian church (for example) is inherently unsafe or suffers from fear as some suggest. Many women are very happy, feel very safe and have a sense of fulfillment in such settings.

The reality is that most abusive stories told relate in some way to male leaders exerting power over women (although recently many stories of male leadership abuse of younger males have emerged). Any theology that could be interpreted as reducing the creative, image-bearing beauty of every human being must be wisely handled, well-tested and understood by those involved to have the potential to be used by dark forces for abusive purposes. This is why wise shepherds must understand perspectives outside of their own echo chambers.

Perhaps these words from Diane Langberg will help:

"Abuse of power is a cancer in the body of Christ. How Christendom uses terminology regarding gender is sometimes an aspect of the disease. We need to let the light of a holy God expose us and our systems. A man named Jesus had nothing to do with these ways. He used his power without abuse, coercion, or complicity. A male named Jesus interacted with all kinds of women and protected, blessed, healed, encouraged and lifted them up. He never told them to submit to evil or wrongdoing. He didn't silence them. Much of masculinity in Christendom looks nothing like Jesus. It has been contaminated by secular culture and sanctioned using theological terms. Any theology that does not produce the fruit of Jesus is false. We are doing great damage to countless vulnerable people and to God's church because people destroyed by abuse perpetrated by the powerful cannot use the fullness of their God-given gifts to bless His body. Those perpetrating the abuse are not gifting the church as

God intended either. We simply keep repeating words almost like a mantra: leader, head, submission, authority, God-ordained. We need to drag into the light those things we cover with familiar and good words and test them to see whether our labels and our applications are of God. Many are not."[5]

Leadership, Submission and Honour

"I was told to attend a training session led by an influential management guru. He was on many websites as an 'advisor'. During one session he told the staff their job was to 'make their pastor look good'. We all had a one-to-one interview in which the expert asked, 'Give me a mark out of ten for how committed you are to the vision of the senior pastor'. A couple of weeks later it was announced that as a result of the feedback from the advisor that all church partners would be asked to attend a course called 'Under Cover' using the material by John Bevere. We all knew the pastor was struggling to find his feet and to be respected and it was now clear who was to blame."

Bevere's book forms part of a huge Christian western leadership industry. Out of the factory come numerous leadership quotes and simplistic sayings that catch on and become mantras in their own right. They may sound right and are often supported by a few verses from the Bible. Here are a few that immediately come to mind:

"Everything rises and falls on leadership," (Maxwell)

becomes "Followers just follow."

"Submission is about being under a mission which is set by the visionary leader" becomes, "The vision is for the leader and the rest just follow."

"Whose covering are you under?" or "Who is your apostle?" becomes, "You won't be blessed if you're not under the covering of an anointed one."

"Don't touch the Lord's anointed," becomes "If you argue, you are rebellious."

"A healthy church is a growing church," becomes, "If the leader leads a growing church, they must be anointed."

The problem with so much of this is that the emphasis is on the power and position of the leader and the rest (followers) are not expected to have answers, solve problems, show the way, to protect others or to have authority. We develop a leadership centric model that is a sitting target for narcissistic and abusive leadership practices. "Honour your leader" easily morphs into extravagance to demonstrate that honour: five-star hotels, Gucci handbags, huge salaries and ministry gifts for "God's man" follow. Pride will run close behind, ready to pounce.

So the catchphrases evolve and toxic, fear-based cultures emerge:

"You are suffering because..." (Creates fear of a lack of faith.)

"If you do what I tell you, you will be blessed…" (Creates fear of decision-making.)

"You do want to obey God, don't you…?" (Creates fear of doing things wrong.)

"If you want to develop your gifts and ministry then…" (Creates fear of not being used.)

Leaders can easily end up shouting "cardiac" in the hope followers hear "heart attack" rather than recognise that the diagnosis of a so-called expert shepherd is wildly inaccurate.

This is not to say that submission, obedience and contentment are not related to our attitudes towards leadership — they are. But we do need to develop a theology of leadership that also includes sacrifice, humility, suffering and servanthood. The whole biblical narrative argues that the power dynamics of religious hierarchy and control have failed and there is an upside-down way of doing Kingdom leadership. Light is shone on a suffering servant whose yoke is easy and whose burden is light rather than the weight of tradition and control imposed by the religious authorities of the day. The language we use and the systems we create must reflect the whole, not just a part. This is wise theology in practice. Wise shepherds lead with their focus on Jesus rather than model themselves on Moses and David! These amazing Old Testament characters can be used to justify all sorts of practices if not understood in the light of Jesus.

"He would accuse people who challenged him of

witchcraft, weak, low-faith, small-minded. I believe that X espoused an extra-biblical theology, giving a sense of legitimacy and support to the senior leader's self-image as an apostolic leader, with a spiritual covering, largely beyond question and reproach i.e. the man with the plan. The organisation became more important than people."

Faith and (Toxic) Positivity

Faith as an experience is difficult to define. It involves trust, hope, belief, the unseen, confidence and even doubt and questions. Christian faith is rooted in the promises of God but is not a simple solution to all of life's challenges. Faith in Jesus is likely to throw up more problems! I have a feeling that what some call faith today bears little resemblance to the faith of the earliest Christ followers whose trust, hope and belief meant allegiance to Christ rather than Caesar or any other person or thing. It was a daily decision to follow Jesus and all the consequences that might follow rather than positive vibes for greater blessing (usually related to good things happening to you). The cross of suffering was likely close behind faith in Jesus.

Faith easily becomes a kind of "live life positively" message, believing that all things are possible and we can do all things through Christ (verses often taken out of context). Christ-centred faith is more to do with contentment and contending in the midst of suffering and pain rather than believing for the next new car, new building, new growth phase, healing or breakthrough (whatever that means). The irony is that unwise faith theology (positive toxicity) has the potential to be a dangerous source of further turmoil rather than healing, provision or breakthrough. It has no room for a wise theology of suffering.

True faith is a source of hope that won't disappoint and trust that gives a sense of peace in the midst of a storm. We know Jesus is in charge and our allegiance and confidence is in Him. This means we are likely to find resilience and strength in troubled times. Faith is not a formula, a spell or a chant. Faith is not walking around a building shouting at demons. Faith does not dismiss, diminish or suppress emotions. Faith doesn't ignore pain. "Everything happens for a reason", "Just pray more and all will be well", "God never gives more than you can handle", "Binding the spirit of despair" and various other mantras can unintentionally make things worse and create guilt for feeling and experiencing continued pain: It's my lack of faith. It is my fault. But God doesn't deal in gaslighting and wise theological leadership won't either. Faith is never a barrier to authenticity but a bridge to it. Wise theology always encourages authenticity, trust and confidence in Christ, knowing that by His Spirit He will give strength, resilience, friends, advisors and so much more if we give Him the space to do what He loves to do. This is not easy faith.

Prophecy and the Prophet

"Out of the blue the call came. The wife of a dear couple we knew well had left her husband for another man. The church was devastated, not least because this couple was a senior pastoral couple and were champions of healthy marriage. A small group decided to pray and had invited the husband to attend a gathering. I was very cautious and unable to attend. I could not stop them meeting but pleaded with the leader not to allow prophetic words that could be interpreted in so many ways. Emotions were high. I managed to change commitments and turned up. 'The Lord is saying it will be OK and she will return. This is the work of the devil and I bind the Spirit of division' (or words to that effect). I knew so much more about the situation than the prophetic voice and I was extremely doubtful that such events would or even could happen. The result was many months of regular conversations trying to work through what God had promised on that night. The prophetic word never materialised and the pain it caused lasted many months."

Words wrapped up as "God has said" and spoken by a so-called prophet or from someone in a position of authority are powerful. They can encourage and comfort but are also used to control and manipulate or so that the speaker can say something that they feel unwilling to talk about in real English face-to-face. We now hear stories of well-known prophets scrolling social media to discover information about people in meetings. The pressure is on to perform and people come expecting to hear from the anointed man or woman of God. Wise theology will understand the power dynamics of prophecy (in whatever form it is understood).

When people are in crisis, pain or suffering from sudden trauma, they are in great need of wisdom but they are also extremely vulnerable. Appeals at the end of a meeting (with cleverly chosen music in the background) that stress breakthrough and that the Lord is saying this or that can be extremely damaging. My appeal is not to restrict or over manage gifts given to the church, but for shepherds to understand the harm being done when sheep are being manipulated by prophecy and power dynamics. Many people do not have the courage, understanding or strength to reject or challenge a so-called word from God.

Forgiveness and Repentance

I am a great fan of Elton John. 'Goodbye Yellow Brick Road' was one of the first albums I ever bought. On the 1976 album, 'Blue Moves', Elton sings, 'Sorry Seems to Be the Hardest Word'. Sadly this has proven to be true in so many stories told about abusive leadership in the church. Victims are told to forgive but those in power seem unable to say a proper sorry. Danielle Strickland put it like this on X (2024):

"I wonder why it's so hard for people who now realise they've been part of harmful systems to just admit it and ask people harmed how to make things right? Confession and restitution are tools every Christian should know! Making wrong things right (even things we've been complicit in) is gospel work. Why does this seem so foreign to people?"

We are good at the sorry if and the sorry but. Most of us don't like to take ownership of mistakes, bad decisions and behaviours. True apologies uncover mistakes and sometimes reveal character issues and leaders have often recoiled from the thought of being uncovered, as they then think of themselves and their position as vulnerable. Real apologies however open the door to real forgiveness. Wise shepherds will help the sheep forgive and not hinder them with ifs and buts.

It is too easy to make forgiveness an escape route from consequences and a quick way to get back on track with the vision. The power holder uses the gift of forgiveness to avoid proper apology and personal responsibility. To help the victim forgive there is a need to know what they are forgiving. Vague thoughts such as "If I've caused pain" do not help. Forgiveness is, of course, a sign of the arrival of God's Kingdom and Jesus shocked His contemporaries when He unconditionally forgave sin and commanded His followers to do the same. Kingdom forgiveness is shocking.

Sadly the idea of unconditional forgiveness can be used by leaders to opt out of personal responsibility for poor behavioural patterns and actions and place the consequential burden on the victim. To make matters worse, the victim can be labelled as bitter and angry if they find forgiveness difficult. Jesus called for repentance as strongly as He called for forgiveness. Wise theology grounds forgiveness in repentance and reconciliation and doesn't use it to avoid consequences for sin.

Vision and Values

Healthy cultures are so important. We all know this. We don't want to feel fear, pressured to perform nor live out false narratives. Culture impacts everything. Culture is more than a set of values on a piece of paper or a clear vision statement. These may help but can be twisted to exert control.

The value of generosity sounds good and is good. We want to be generous and we want the church to be generous. It is a God quality. But when leaders use generosity to manipulate people to give more even when they are struggling to pay the bills or to create standards or unwritten laws that people are expected to abide by, then we have a problem. Is this not what the Pharisees did? They added to the law their own interpretations of the law. Generosity can also be used as an excuse to pay excessive salaries or ministry gifts to "mates". Well verbalised and written values don't equal healthy cultures.

"The senior leader was struggling to understand why I had not moved house to be nearer to the church. This, of course, would be helpful to all. I had a mortgage to pay and no commitment from the church for longer term employment. We all 'worked for Jesus' so had to act according to the 'faith' value. I wasn't moving because I lacked faith and therefore wasn't embracing the values of the church. A short while later, my salary was cut in half without proper process. I was glad I hadn't succumbed to the pressure. I resigned a few weeks later. A healthy value had become an unhealthy culture."

We could pick further wonderful and healthy theological and organisational values and discuss how they can be twisted so as to manipulate and control. Unity easily morphs into uniformity and a "believe what I believe". Holiness becomes an unhealthy purity culture where dress codes and relationship standards are enforced.

Mission and Growth

All churches want to grow. We like to see lives changed and more people experiencing the transforming grace of God in their lives. We can easily argue this from Scripture. The Kingdom of God advances and Jesus continues to call people to Himself. The concern that some have raised in their stories is that numbers become the driver and the major measure of success. As long as the front door is bigger and income is increasing to cover growing demands, all is well. No-one really asks why the backdoor is so big! Things look and sound great but as W.E. Deming states in 'The New Economics', "Wherever there is fear, there will be wrong numbers."

Mission is important. Many churches need to recapture the urgency of the day, but in the hands of unwise shepherds what was meant for good is turned to harm. The growth and success of the organisation is all that matters and the systems created to make it happen take over. Growth keeps the hungry system happy and the pastor becomes a CEO of a business with all the leadership theory and practice that goes with it rather than the pastor of a community. We must handle finances well, we need to create good systems but wise enough not to allow people to become the target of a marketing department or a fundraising campaign with all its targets!

"I was responsible for all community services, tasked to find opportunities for people to serve. However many I came up with which were meeting genuine needs in the local community weren't offered to people if we couldn't stamp our branding all over it. Only things which could be clearly labelled as being done by our church, even though they had negligible impact on the needs of the community, were deemed OK."

One of the favourite sayings heard at many a conference has been, "A healthy church is a growing church", therefore if your church is growing it must be healthy and have a great leader. Growing bodies can, of course, hide a range of severe and life-threatening diseases. Too many churches have found this to be the case as the cancers of spiritual, financial, physical and emotional abuse have been revealed below the surface of considerable growth. It is quite possible to hide behind size, growth and systems for a long time. Wise theology asks questions of the backdoor — not just rejoicing in the front door — and seeks to find measures for health in character, discipleship and Christlikeness — not just numbers on a piece of paper.

Go First to Your Brother or Sister

"If your brother or sister sins, go and point out their fault, just between the two of you. If they listen to you, you have won them over. But if they will not listen, take one or two others along, so that 'every matter may be established by the testimony of two or three witnesses.' If they still refuse to listen, tell it to the church; and if they refuse to listen even to the church, treat them as you would a pagan or a tax collector" (Matthew 18:15–17).

"I couldn't believe the phone call. He wanted to go see the victim's father to try and explain what happened and to seek forgiveness. Not only was the case with the police at the time but the father would probably have killed him! The argument used sounded so righteous, 'I want to follow what the Bible says'. It lacked common sense, broke the law and was unhelpful to the victim and their family."

This story (or similar) has been repeated again and again with Matthew 18:15–16 used by leaders to justify unwise and manipulative behaviours. The victim is accused of being rebellious and gossiping by going to outside organisations or individuals. The context of this passage is causing harm to "little ones" and rescuing lost sheep. It is about ordinary believers dealing with conflict caused by sin, not a methodology to challenge elders and pastors who have used their power to abuse the vulnerable. 1 Timothy 5:19–21 talks specifically about "overbearing" leaders. It is also clear that the power in-balance is huge and going one-to-one is potentially dangerous and likely harmful. It is easy for a leader to use such meetings to cover up, deny, minimise, blame, manipulate and gaslight. Such behaviours display the opposite heart encouraged by Jesus in seeking out the one and caring for the "little ones". Wise theology always looks at context, considers the weak and looks for justice. Using Scripture as a weapon as some have done is in itself an appalling abuse.

Wise theology is not the same as perfect theology! Wise theology is all about asking tough questions of one another and our actions in the light of the whole of Scripture. It requires continuous learning and understanding. Wise shepherds will read, and will develop their understanding of people and pastoral issues. They will go out of their comfort zone to develop actions that reflect the whole counsel of God, not just the part that they are comfortable with. This takes commitment, honesty, integrity, transparency and candid conversation. This leads us nicely into an overview of Psychological Safety and Courageous Followership which will draw us into a new, wiser and safer story.

BETTER THAN THIS

DAVID WARREN

Interlude 2
Psychological Safety

Fear often lurks behind power: fear of failure, mistakes, opinions, disagreement, causing upset, creating division, humiliation and shame. Fear will inevitably create a culture where silence is common and silence will breed uncertainty, insecurity and abuse. We see this pattern time and again in the church, in business, government and the arts. An authoritative voice, an amazing gift or a position of power have become sources of appalling cultural and behavioural patterns. Fear begets abuse.

Fear will also lead to the creation of echo chambers where only echo voices are listened to. All other voices have been silenced or have run away. It is only when people realise that their voice was not the only anti-echo voice, that enough power is gathered to challenge the system. Sometimes this takes years, a terrible event or the death of an abuser.

"People were controlled by being deemed people in or out of favour, the chosen ones, where some were 'in' (the echo chamber) and they could do no wrong, and if you came into conflict with them (anti-echo voice) you were automatically in the wrong, despite the circumstances. You were then subject to gaslighting to keep you wanting to be in the 'in' group."

The scripture "Perfect love drives out fear" (1 John

4:18) is perhaps one of the best known verses in the Bible. Love overcomes fear. If the church is to be a reflection of a God who is love, it must aim to be a fearless community, a psychologically safe community. This is no new idea. As early as 1965 Edgar Schein discussed how psychologically safe cultures helped people cope with organisational uncertainty and change. In the 1990s Amy Edmondson (Harvard Business School) developed and popularised the theme.[6] To her surprise she discovered that those health teams that reported the most errors had the highest positive outcomes. Something was happening in those teams that created a culture where mistakes were talked about, highlighted and learnt from. In 2015 Google carried out what became "Project Aristotle" which analysed team performance, behaviours and outcomes. It discovered that where psychological safety was present in a team, it would outperform other teams even if they had less talented or experienced people in them. What if the church prioritised developing safe cultures rather than gifted cultures? It sounds more like the Bible image of the body of Christ.

Amy Edmondson identifies the benefits and challenges of creating fearless cultures and suggests ways in which everyone can help foster such cultures. To understand how all this works we need to investigate the world we live in in a bit more detail. Hold tight. You are part of this world.

We live in a VUCA world and the church and all its members aren't immune. It impacts everything and everyone. A leader sneezes in Australia and pastors are reacting in the United Kingdom within minutes. We can't hide from it and we are foolish if we don't seek to understand it better. This is why people know more, hear more and see more than ever before. We might not like it, but people are empowered and often confused by information — more than ever before. It is no wonder that news of abuse has caused so many issues when the church covers up, fails to communicate and deliver what it promises. Bad news travels far and fast.

Volatile

A bank collapses in the USA and instantaneously interest rates rise in the UK, and we are facing huge economic challenges. War breaks out in Ukraine and in a matter of hours food prices rise. A computer update goes badly, and NHS computers crash, and your appointment is cancelled. It is all so sudden. We are all thrown into the mix and we can feel that everything is out of our control. Changes and events happen fast and continuously, and they impact us all. Quickly.

Uncertain

The world looks and feels uncertain and so predicting the future is increasingly difficult. What we thought would happen tomorrow or next week may be suddenly halted because of an event on the other side of the world. Investing in and the sharing of information can help.

Complex

The world is more interconnected and interdependent than ever before. Systems are more complex and leadership hierarchy is reduced. It isn't always obvious why things happen and who makes the decisions that are behind events. Teams must interact instantaneously, candidly and easily.

Ambiguous

With ever increasing information comes different and conflicting interpretations of that information. Often it is not clear whether the information we read is true or made up using AI! We just might discover we made a decision based on false information. We are conned by clever scams and overwhelmed by choice.

What does all this VUCA stuff have to do with you, the church and psychological safety? It is clear that open and honest communication is vital. We need to be flexible, creative and feel able to share ideas and opinions so as to value one another and what everyone brings to the table. If we do not feel safe and we don't respond well the VUCA world will likely fuel abusive cultures. It is an unseen power. The church cannot hide bad news in the way it did, people are empowered with information more than ever before and victims from other sides of the world can easily find one another and tell their stories. Trust in leadership has been eroded, stories of abusive leadership are told in Australia one minute and read by thousands in the UK the next. The influence of powerful leaders easily spreads around the globe but when they fail and fall the impacts are huge and the analysis intense. All this is a result of the unseen power of the VUCA world.

Psychologically safe churches will be creative and respond quickly to unexpected challenges, communication will be candid and mistakes admitted and learnt from. There will be a culture of natural and strong accountability. People will be able to share concerns and raise questions and therefore feel valued and listened to. There will be a diversity of input which will help build a community from every tribe, tongue and nation. There will be no space for echo-chambers, superstars or hidden agendas. Churches committed to being psychologically safe will cut the power of the abusive dynamics revealed in the numerous stories told in this book and elsewhere. This will be a community well placed to be healthy in our VUCA world.

One factor, however, remains a constant in all this. However flat, organisational hierarchy leaders will have the greatest influence on the culture of a church. They hold the most power and are likely to be the most talked about person in the church (it took me some years to recognise that reality). In a world gone VUCA-mad, how can church leaders foster fearless, safe cultures? Research by such folks as Amy Edmundson suggests the following are vital:

- Encourage open dialogue: Leaders expect and ask for questions, listen to doubts and share in discussions and are open about their own questions, admitting to their own mistakes. All our faith stories are different and we are always learning from them.

- Empathetic listening: Leaders are expected to provide answers and sometimes live with the heavy burden of feeling they have to give answers. Everyone needs to listen without immediate judgment and giving simplistic faith answers. Empathy allows people to feel heard and validated and will reduce the guilt of questions, failures, doubts and fears. Leaders are no different. If followers would listen to leaders and vice versa, then understanding would increase and trust is built. We may not agree but we can understand.
- Everyone vulnerable: When church leaders model vulnerability — by sharing their own struggles or questions — they set an example. This breaks down any perceived power and hierarchical barriers and demonstrates that everyone is a work in progress. Psychologically safe communities are fundamentally learning communities. The most important question becomes, what did you learn, not what did you do wrong.
- Emphasise grace not standards: We communicate that people belong, not because they are good but because they are part of a family where everyone is imperfect. People will not be vulnerable about their own imperfections until they feel safe to share them. If leaders come across as perfect people with perfect lives,

then false pictures are projected.
- Enjoy diverse voices: Small groups, discussion panels, or one-on-one mentorship programs can offer spaces where people from diverse backgrounds feel free to share without fear of group judgment. This helps people experience psychological safety within smaller, trusted communities.
- Equip and support leaders: Psychologically safe leadership teams are always learning. Training on emotional intelligence, conflict resolution, mental health or trauma awareness all say, "We are wanting to be and do things better!"
- Excel in handling conflict: Conflict is inevitable in any community. Handling it with respect, understanding and compassion will reinforce psychological safety, and will demonstrate that disagreement doesn't mean rejection.

None of these are easy and all take commitment and courage. It involves candid conversations, high accountability, low control and high authenticity. Too many of the stories told in this book and elsewhere speak of leaders expecting people to follow without understanding basic principles of human behaviours and interactions. Jesus calls the religious leaders of His day "hypocrites" (mask-wearers) and sadly many of us as leaders have worn too many masks and then wonder why things go horribly wrong. Psychologically safe churches consign the masks to the bin marked "rubbish".

It is important to recognise that psychologically safe cultures are not the same as polite, nice, friendly, mate cultures. They will not allow team members to get away with dangerous, harmful behaviours nor will they accept poor performance.

The following rehashed story illustrates it well:

"I was devastated and privileged to be asked to preside over the funeral of a young man who had committed suicide as a result of serious depression. It posed so many questions for me about hell and eternal torment as prescribed by the statement of faith in our denomination. I wrestled with this for many months discovering that the early church may well have believed something very different from what I had assumed to be true. I kept it silent as any hint of any form of universalism would inevitably cause huge issues for me. Would I be sacked? Would I be labelled a heretic? I had no idea how to share with my fellow elders, let alone the trustees and fellow denominational leaders I considered as friends. I was fearful. What was I to do as I began to understand Patristic Universalism (God will not abandon nor forsake His beloved creation and all will be reconciled to Him through repentance at some point either now or in eternity) as a biblically and historically reasonable standpoint whilst knowing that others had no concept of such thinking" (Sophie's story).

Fear! Fear of sharing new concepts, different ideas and real concerns. Fear of consequences, reactions and assumptions.

With a basic understanding of psychological safety and wise theology, things would have been so different for the Sophie's of this world, if the culture of their faith community had been safe and fearless skills would have been recognised, doubts listened to, opinions valued (if not always agreed with) and conflict handled gracefully. It would not have been an easy ride but it would have been healthy for all. It might be worth reading Sophie's story and asking yourself what Sophie should have reasonably expected from her leaders.

Amy Edmundson created seven statements to assess how psychologically safe a team might be (I have altered and shortened them for the sake of space!) and I hope they might provide a framework into which you can place your team.

1. If you make a mistake, it is not held against you.
2. Members are able to bring up problems and tough issues.
3. People accept others for being different.
4. It is safe to take a risk.
5. It is easy to ask for help.
6. No one will deliberately undermine the effort of others.
7. Unique skills, abilities and strengths are recognised and valued.

DAVID WARREN

Interlude 3
Courageous Followership

Over the years I have sat through hundreds of leadership seminars, listened to numerous podcasts and read many "how to be a great leader" books. Many helpful books remain on my bookshelf. I have an MA in Missional Leadership and have tried my hardest to be the best leader I possibly could be.

In many respects I am no different from many of my contemporaries. We have been part of a huge leadership industry developed mainly in the USA. Perhaps it can all be summed up by a famous phrase used by the evangelical leadership guru, John Maxwell: "Everything rises and falls on leadership."[7] Much of what I have learnt has been helpful but it seems to me the jury is out as to how successful all this huge investment of time, energy, money and personnel has been. Are churches led more effectively now than they were? Are churches more effective as Jesus communities now than they were back then? The evidence is not as clear-cut as we might like it to be. Over my lifetime many new churches, groups, streams and networks have emerged but overall the "western" church congregations have shrunk and Christian influence declined.

Some of the most influential leadership figures have also hit the buffers of scandal and abuse (Bill Hybells,

Brian Houston, Mike Pilavachi, Ravi Zacarias to name but four who have influenced my leadership thinking). Something has gone terribly wrong. Perhaps Rusty Ricketson summarizes Maxwell's work the best: "Followers cannot sufficiently navigate on their own; leaders accomplish tasks (and) followers cannot navigate on their own, leaders navigate for them."[8]

I suggest that the power, importance and the potential positive contribution of followership has been largely neglected. Followers become by-products and doers of the vision and strategy set by leaders and the focus of attention has become the charisma, gift, presence and performance of leaders. This is a recipe for disaster and a root of many issues highlighted in the stories told in this book and elsewhere. We need a fresh understanding of what it means to be a courageous follower in the light of a rapidly changing culture and a wise theology of leadership.

The rise of social media, expanding social networks, increased availability of information, the breakdown of traditional hierarchies such as family and the failed models of Christian leadership have resulted in a declining respect for leaders. Relationship has become more important than hierarchy or organisational labels. The gap between leader and follower has decreased whilst the follower is also more emboldened and knowledgeable than ever. Robert Kelley goes further:

"We tend to think of leaders as the proactive 'cause'

and followership as the reactive 'effect'. But what if the opposite were true? Are leadership attitudes, behaviours and performance more a result of followership than the other way around? For example, do sheep produce a particular style of leadership, regardless of the leader's personality or disposition? Many leaders are malleable products of cumulative followership actions."[9]

Could followers determine who will be accepted as a leader and whether or not that leader will be effective, safe and able to create fearless cultures? If that is the case we need courageous followers more than ever before. Let's explore in some detail what wise theology might contribute to this discussion before asking what a courageous follower looks like.

Every Christian is a follower of Christ and a cursory read of the gospels reveal Jesus was first and foremost a follower. The Christian leadership industry has often made leadership the goal of followership, a bit like a promotional hierarchy. We start on the coffee rota then move to the kids team or youth worker, then jump to assistant pastor, associate pastor, senior pastor and then (if your church grows big enough) an apostle or prophet (vastly generalised of course). The greatest honour is reserved for the apostle and followership easily becomes a means to an end. Wise theology creates a very different picture.

Genesis 1–2 paints a beautiful picture of harmony. Eve helped Adam. Adam and Eve walked closely with one another and intimately with God. There is oneness. Humanity is at ease with itself, with God and with creation. The command to "subdue" and "have dominion over" creation (Genesis 1:28) is given to the whole of humanity. In Psalm 72 "radah" (dominion) is used to describe Godly Kingly rule as one who protects the defenceless and provides justice to the poor and oppressed. Humanity demonstrates Godly followership and leadership when it rules with care and fairness always seeking oneness.

The prophetic literature of the Old Testament highlights justice and righteousness and challenges leaders who act in ways that are contrary to God's ways. Peace (shalom) is achieved as people walk closely with God and intimately with one another. The fall distorted both leadership and followership. Adam and Eve became rebellious followers and Godly leadership over creation was corrupted. Oneness destroyed. Jesus comes as both the perfect example of followership and leadership. He trusts and obeys the Father as Prophet, Priest and King and then prays, "that they (followers of Jesus) may all be one, just as You, Father are in Me, and I in You, that they may be in Us, so that the world may believe" (John 17:21). Here we have a picture of restored oneness. Christ-centred followership and leadership both seek restoration. The church is called to continue this ministry of reconciliation and pursue the restoration of all things.

When we read the New Testament we soon discover that pictures or metaphors rather than labels and titles are used to describe how the church should function: body, mother and child and bride, to name but three. It's about responsibility, affection and relationship rather than title and hierarchy. There is little room for separate categories of leader and follower as leadership functions in the context of the shared community of followers. Everyone stands and moves around in a circle rather than having a position on a pyramid. This all led Banks and Ledbetter to conclude:

"As far as the usual terms for secular offices, only one of the more than thirty (offices) that existed in the first century appears in Paul's writings, but it is used exclusively of the governing role played by Christ in the Church" (Colossians 1:18).[10]

The focus is community, not leadership. Even the words used for "elder" and "overseer" are verbs rather than nouns. Everyone is a brother or co-worker. Leaders walk alongside rather than above or over as so much of the leadership language used today suggests. Leonard Sweet puts it like this:

"I hope to convince you to quit defining yourself as a leader, stop aspiring after leadership, and instead set your sights on being a 'Jesus follower' or 'first follower'. I hope to convince you, instead of inviting others to come under your leadership, to invite them into a fellowship of followers, a ragtag band of pilgrims bound for the promised land."[11]

My contention is that courageous followership provides the third key element to creating safe, fearless church cultures. Followers (all of us) have far more potential for healthy influence than we imagine and all of us need to take this responsibility more seriously and quieten the all too powerful "leadership is everything" voice. You can make a difference but sometimes it will take a bit of courage. Your followership plays a vital role in an organisation. Your thinking, your creativity, your gift, you as a person are important. When we get this right, followership becomes leadership and leadership becomes followership. Risk is reduced, poor leadership challenged and effectiveness increased. We cannot afford to miss out!

"I listened to the story of a friend who was a core leader in a thriving church. The senior leader was well-known, extremely gifted and a loyal friend to many. He had collected too many roles and responsibilities and his diary was crammed. He thrived on busyness. My friend was worried so he went to speak to the leader in an attempt to challenge these unhealthy behaviours. He didn't know that two others had done the same but none had communicated with the others. About six months later the leader admitted to having an affair with a member of the congregation. The results were devastating for so many. I wonder to this day what would have happened if those three influential followers had pressed the 'stop' button when it was clear there were issues. They had the power to do it. They had the knowledge to do it."

So what does a courageous follower look like and how does it work?

In so many stories, reports, news items and social media feeds one thing stands out. Key followers and other leaders knew. They had heard the rumour, seen an incident, experienced some pain, were concerned about actions, language or the way things were handled. Why did no-one do anything about it? There are many answers to this question, some of which have already been answered (others not) but after mulling it all over I have come to the conclusion some in influential "follower" or technical roles, such as trustees, followed badly and tried to protect themselves or the organisation. They were living in psychological unsafe places. They mixed up submission, gift, growth, friendship, anointing or supposed success with good followership. Some lacked courage despite being in important and influential positions. The real victims rarely have the power, courage or emotional strength to challenge at the time of the abuse, but others have no excuse and end up covering up and protecting themselves and their leader (mate). Many victims become courageous followers as little by little they pluck up the courage to tell their stories, refusing to listen to unwise theology and succumbing to further power manipulation. Followers become leaders and courage confronts darkness.

Those who have looked into the dynamics of leader-follower relationships have often come up with descriptive models of followership. Ira Chalef[12] and Robert Kelley[13] are two such writers and their models form the foundation of my comments. My hope is that I have made it study-light, story-strong and relevant to everyone in all church settings.

Over the years I've had the joy of working alongside many amazing people. Their commitment, generosity, sacrifice and kindness have been outstanding and at times awe-inspiring. The church is made up of millions of such people. Unfortunately the dynamic between leader and follower (it is difficult not to use such terms) has often gone array due to unwise theology, controlling behaviours, power in-balance and sometimes poor, even poisonous followership.

I hate putting people into boxes. None of us fit square shapes. Sometimes, however, categories can help us think through issues, open up conversations and challenge our thinking. This is the intention of what follows. Give your mind permission to be challenged about yourself, your leadership, your church commitment and your values. Please do not box yourself or others in!

Passive Followers

These folks demonstrate little self-motivation or critical thinking. It is the leader's job to motivate them to complete a task and the leader's job to do all the thinking. In church life this person easily lets you down on a Sunday having promised to do the coffee. The excuses often have a sense of the bazaar about them. They will do just about enough to be considered part of the family just in case the family ever needed to support them. They may well blame the leader for not caring even if it was their woeful decision that led them into a mess they now want out of. These folks are immensely frustrating to leaders as they drain resources, sap energy and are rarely thankful: unless, of course, the leader actually succeeds in motivating them.

Conformist Followers

These folks exhibit little critical thinking. They are delightfully positive about doing tasks of various kinds. The job of the leader is to set the vision and make the decisions and the conformist will enthusiastically follow. Controlling leaders love these kinds of people because they are able to use them for their own ends. These are the folks to call if you want a job done — any job, any time, any place. I would suggest that many young interns in big churches are chosen if they exhibit the traits of a conformist follower. Who wants a feisty, argumentative, opinionated intern? This is why the stories of burn out, bullying and abuse are often found in such faith spaces. Wise theology and wise leaders will want to encourage and expect critical thinking, questioning and candid conversations rather than close them down.

Alienated Followers

These folks do think for themselves but often their negative behaviours are rooted in anger or hurt.

They may be completely unaware that they are being controlled by history. In church life, this will emerge as they actively resist new ideas as unworkable. They are quick to point out when the music is too loud, the preaching too long, the coffee too strong or the new carpet is the wrong colour. They are the ones who post a brown envelope through the pastor's door on a Sunday afternoon. Their attitude creates alienation and antagonism between leader, follower and most other people in the group. Their opinion will be heard. The trouble is that these folks are often gifted and think they know their Bible. Their bitterness can be rooted in the fact that previous church leaders have fallen out with them and they are never able to realise that their own behaviours are the issue, not bullying, coercive, controlling leaders. These folks do not require high levels of support (they are independent) but they are likely to provide very high levels of challenge as they act out their independence and speak out of their pain.

Pragmatic Followers

These folks are often quite cautious and will often feel the need to watch and assess before joining in or making a commitment. They may never come across as "fully in" and might be described as bystanders by some leaders who would want or expect more from them. They won't rock the boat unless really pressed to do so, do not need a lot of support and are not a challenge. They will do what they will do and help where they will help. In church life, these are the folks who fill the pews, make up the numbers, watch the show and join in when it seems reasonable to do so. They are important to those leaders who like their numbers, performance and stage. They are no trouble, often give some finances and will likely be there and enjoy it. If everything looks good, sounds good and feels good, then everything will be just fine.

Implementing Followers

These folks have a can-do attitude. They are the kinds of people that every leader loves to have on their team as they will cheer them on, support them, strengthen their hand and go the extra mile on behalf of the organisation. They are highly supportive and create very few challenges. They are often really good, gifted, creative and productive people. The wise leader will not be surprised if these folks are labelled "yes men or women" by some and will understand that a team of such folks will form dangerous echo-chambers and may even become part of the toxic, abusive cultures. In a church setting, these followers will instinctively support their leader, believe their story and therefore create defensive narratives. They will find it difficult to believe they are part of the illness and even contribute to an abusive culture. It may take many years, yet another crisis or undeniable evidence to change their thinking and face up to reality. They may well continue to use unwise theology to defend their position. They are extremely supportive and provide few challenges.

Courageous (Exemplary) Followers

These folks think for themselves, will take responsibility for their own actions, are actively involved, positive and demonstrate a can-do attitude. They support the mission of the organisation rather than the vision of a leader and therefore challenge and question decisions and ideas that are detrimental to the organisation or unhealthy for the leader. They are not always easy team members but in a church setting, they are vital if cultures are to be safe and fearless. They will be willing to sacrifice their own popularity and even put friendships at risk for the sake of the mission (Christ-centred churches).

I can hear some readers thinking, "Ah, yes! That is Mrs Smith or Mr Jones." Please be careful. Perhaps we have all fitted into one or more of these categories at some point or another and we may well have been part of the problem. We just might be Mrs Smith or Mr Jones!

So What Does Courage Look Like?

Many of you will be facing daunting challenges right now, others will have their stories of how God gave them the courage to act, speak, change or make a decision despite everything in you saying "You can't do this!" Fear grips us all in different ways and so courage looks different for all of us. For some the thought of confrontation is traumatic and to be avoided if at all possible. For some, not least because they are convinced they are anointed and chosen by God, admitting mistakes and apologising can be a huge challenge, whilst for others change can trigger physical and emotional fear. Saying "no" can be hugely problematic for many. Courage is difficult to describe or tie down and at times you will only know when you need courage.

Biblical courage is deeply rooted in spiritual conviction. We are sure that what God has said, commanded or promised is so important that we place our trust in Him rather than succumb to fear. As we move forward, we discover enough grace to face the challenge. Such courage is for everyone and there is no differentiation between leader and follower. For someone to talk to a stranger or for a young lady to challenge a powerful male leader (even by talking to a friend about it) who has sent inappropriate texts, takes huge courage. Christlike courage is for every follower of Christ, but the reality is that courage is often easier to muster when you have the power and position as a leader. Abusive leaders take advantage of this power in-balance.

Every Christlike follower will look to exhibit and develop courage. It isn't easy and for victims of abusive cultures it is incredibly difficult. God's way of getting alongside these folk is to give them friends, people advocates or specialist organisations. Through these, God gives courage. John describes the Holy Spirit as an advocate who comes alongside to help ("parakletos"). When leaders get alongside and help victims, they set an example as Christ-followers first. If their character is not consistently displaying courageous follower traits, the red flag is flying.

Courageous leaders and followers will:

Serve People

"Every couple of months I met with our church advisor. He was so helpful and often challenged my mindset. I described a growing church and use of my time. I dropped in that I spent a couple of hours each week cleaning the carpet. He looked at me and said, 'That needs to stop as the church is too big now and you should have others to do it for you.' It bothered me. I never stopped cleaning the carpet each week."

Any sense that someone is too important to do a job is a red flag to be resisted. One church leader I know expected all staff to be accountable to one another for acts of people ministry (preaching, teaching, Bible study, praying, visiting), leadership ministry (training, coaching, mentoring, vision and strategy) and practical ministry (cleaning, serving food) each week. I like this.

Act With Integrity

This may mean risking rejection and voicing discomfort with requests being made by those in power. Integrity matters most and it all links back to psychological safety. Courageous followers value conscience.

Be Loyal

Change happens and leaders need to lead and make decisions. Change creates uncertainty and in these times courageous followership looks like loyalty and is usually healthy for yourself and the church. We may not like all aspects of change, but sometimes it really doesn't matter that much.

Take Action

It is not uncommon for an abusive leader to ask people to do things, say things or keep silent when the right thing to do is to say no or speak out. To speak out is uncomfortable and requires courage and may well mean reporting to someone else or seeking advice which can then be misinterpreted as gossip or undermining. Hold fast to that which is good.

Take Responsibility

When there are issues and challenges to be faced, a courageous follower will be part of the solution and seek creative ways to help, cheer on and support. You might not have the answer but you can send a text, write a card or make a call.

Speak to Power

Courage may mean speaking to people you do not know or have little connection with. In a denomination or group it might mean a call to the area leader, apostle or overseer. Be factual, be clear, do not blame, make up stories, decide guilt, be rude, nor use the term "everyone is". Report, ask for a response and follow up. If unsure, it is OK to seek advice.

Listen to the Powerless

Safe, fearless cultures will be listening cultures. Leaders will listen to followers and followers to leaders. Leaders then become followers and followers become leaders. Those who have suffered abuse or have lived in toxic culture land may well take time to gather the courage to become courageous followers but if other followers have the courage to listen, then little by little courage spreads.

Courageous followership sounds like listening, integrity, speaking up, speaking out, responsibility and loyalty. It is difficult to define, not easy to "pluck up" and often very allusive. It reads like the stories I told. It often resides not in the powerful but in the powerless, not in the label but in the character and not on the stage but in the pew. Courageous followership is Christ in action. It is the "everything" of the woman at the well, the lady with bleeding and a hated man up a sycamore tree. And the Holy Spirit comes alongside to help in time of need.

Epilogue

Wise theology, psychological safety and courageous followership intersect and overlap. Each interlude has had its own unique flavour but common phrases, ideas and behaviours have emerged. When these are knitted together, they form a three-chord strand that will be extremely difficult to break. It can be used to pull out the dark threads that have entangled too many churches and Christian organisations for too long. This is not a recipe for an easy life, nor a comfortable church, but it will be a safer, wiser, more courageous church for everyone. It will be a church where victims are heard, where listening and learning are everywhere and where abusive leaders and others are held to account. Mistakes will be made and abuse will still happen as we all struggle to live in this broken and straining creation. One day the trees of the field will really clap their hands as we all (everything) go out with joy!

And so let's write a new story as we know we are better than this!

DAVID WARREN

Part Three:
The New Story

The book of Revelation has been interpreted in so many ways over the years. It's been used to defend political standpoints, excuse war and predict end times and dates.

The characters in this extraordinary story have been linked to presidents and dictators, credit cards and vaccines. People have made life decisions based on unwise theological interpretation of the events, numbers, beasts and times as they read into the text. I am sure that John's narrative must speak to today's church in much the same way as it spoke to the seven churches at the time of writing. Revelation still poses the question (amongst others), "How should the Church respond to the culture and powers of the day in a way that reflects the centrality of the risen Christ and the promise of shalom and future restoration of all things in a new heaven and new earth?" The church can look and sound too much like Babylon. Team Lamb is supposed to be very different from Team Dragon.

Babylon (part of "team dragon") is the source of pride, power, exploitation and greed and the seven churches were, like the church today, in danger of becoming too Babylonian. Jesus was no longer their first love nor the centre of their attention. The Christ-following communities were to be centres of worship, justice, generosity, care for the widow and orphan, courageously embodying the way of Christ. The stories I have told in this book (and the hundreds of others told elsewhere) are ones where the church has prioritised wealth, power, control and comfort that inevitably results in abuse, cover-up, mismanagement and controlling practices. Babylon has taken over and Revelation calls the Bride back to the Groom!

As we move into setting the stage on which the new story is to be played out, we must keep the end game in view and once again seek to be a kingdom of people radically different from the Babylon that is our culture. The new enacted story must root out pride and power and seek to display heaven on earth — a people of shalom, justice and care where the "othered" are welcomed. This has profound implications in terms of spiritual abuse, leadership principles and pastoral practices.

We can only ever enact a new story as we all have a fresh vision of the big narrative of a new heaven and earth and realise we are what McKnight calls "dissident disciples"[14] called to be peacemakers, not only for the world but in the church. We must be experts of the "in the church" before we earn the right to complain about the world. We are to be the Everything of chapter 1!

Writing A New Story

Every church is unique. Location, history, size, age range et al. are all going to impact the culture of the church. Some will have many staff but most will have none or a lone pastor. All will rely on many hours of volunteering. Both small and large churches are vulnerable to spiritual abuse in one form or another although the headlines tend to be when the "big name" falls. The characters who play their part in this new story are in every church.

And so to the new story. It is not a leadership story. It is an "everyone's" story in which we all play a part (1 Corinthians 12:12). The characters bounce off one another and will need to improvise and create as they move towards the climax of the story. The cast is incredibly diverse and therefore it is unlikely to be a smooth ride. Mistakes will be made. It is all being acted out in a broken, groaning creation but the cast are all looking forward and acting in anticipation of something far, far better.

I recognise that planning and strategy are important, but we don't need another leadership guide or a new five-point plan. There are enough of them and sadly some have been the source and cause of great pain. The new story is about the creation of fearless, safe church cultures, not about more effective mission and growth strategies. I am not convinced we need yet another "new" church model and history tells me that the newest idea is often a remodelling of a very old idea. A fearless, safe church will make a difference to people whatever its design, theological perspective or style. Get the basics right and much else will follow.

With this in mind, I want to introduce you to the characters that will all play a part in writing and performing this new story. The way these characters interact, think and act will reflect what we have learnt from the old story and the interludes. You will identify with some characters more than others, but you are there in the cast somewhere. The challenge is to play our part to the very best of our ability so that the play is so breathtaking to watch, others will want to jump onto the stage and join in. This is our mission.

The Cast of the New Story

The Director

He makes it all work together. He is the designer, master and creator of the stage and chooses the characters. He can see the play as a whole and will make sure everything comes together. He places the characters but allows them to be themselves (he knows them better than they think). He has enough grace to handle all the craziness but he won't let people get away with poor performance forever. Somehow he works it together for good and in the end, the play will be spectacular. If the characters keep their eyes on him they will find all the grace, patience, courage and composure they need. He seems to have the ability to empower the characters.

Sometimes a messy rehearsal must stop so as to gaze upon the director, whose name is Jesus.

Mr System

Without Mr System, there is chaos and that will create a culture and an organisation very vulnerable to abuse in all its forms. When Mr System grows, he becomes more complex and will tend to control rather than support other cast members as they act out their parts safely and without fear. Mr System creates ways to report and manage the behind-the-scenes mechanisms that make the play smooth, and to follow up on challenges and complaints. Salaries are paid, legalities are followed, contracts are written and the processes of accountability set so that the potential for scandal and intrigue is reduced to a minimum. Sometimes Mr System will frustrate other members of the cast as he can be a bit fussy and pedantic. All the cast must remind themselves that Mr System protects them and those who will one day join the gang!

Mrs Accountability

The more open, honest and transparent Mrs Accountable is the better. She should be easy to handle, positive and supportive. She wants everyone to perform to their very best ability so at times she can point out mistakes, challenge poor actions, behaviours and destructive words. Mrs Accountability keeps the whole cast on the narrow path to peace and safety. She is tough on secrecy and silence. Some of the cast might find Mrs Accountability a bit intrusive, controlling or over demanding. This can be the case if she is over-zealous but everyone needs to be aware that when Mrs Accountability is undermined by anyone, it may be a sign of something rotten under the surface.

Miss Trust

Once established in her role, Miss Trust is wonderful. There is a sense of security and openness that is difficult to describe or analyse. Miss Trust is just there! If she is hurt, damaged or goes absent then serious issues will emerge that may well require close examination. This can be painful for all, as everyone is impacted by a sense of nervousness, anxiety and fear. The cast worry if they are performing up to standard or whether another member is really as supportive as they say they are. This opens the door to silence and sin. Miss Trust is powerful, wonderful, fragile and easily broken. She needs to be taken good care of.

Mr Overcomer

For this actor to overcome what he has suffered, he must be listened to. If unheard, he could become an agitator or protester and that would be the fault of other actors, not him. Mr Overcomer — who used to be Mr Victim — is braver than might be imagined and will often receive extra power and grace from Mr Director. If these prior victims are ignored or cast aside, a toxic culture is almost certainly hiding below the surface and will inevitably damage other actors and lead to many other Mr Victims emerging. Treat Mr Overcomer with grace so that it will spread and the cast will be known as a community of peace. This won't be an easy process as sometimes the trauma and pain will go deep and healing could sound a bit chaotic at times.

Miss Candid

Miss Candid might, at times, seem a bit harsh, uncaring or even rude. She is essential if the team is to function together smoothly and accountability is to be effective. There is nothing worse to Miss Candid than cast members failing to do what they say or being too lazy to learn their words. Honest conversations are essential as long as they do not become personal, harsh or unforgiving. Miss Candid must be quick to apologise if she oversteps the mark. Miss Candid asks tough questions, spots potential weaknesses and areas where doors to abusive behaviours may have been opened. She is willing to take the risk! Safe, fearless cultures are not risk-free.

Lady Pastor (note that Major Leader and Lady Pastor are different characters)

Lady Pastor looks, smells and acts like a shepherd. The cast talk to her, feel safe to share their pain and can trust her to have their best interests at heart. She will help find ways to heal and restore. These skills are crucial as the cast are far from being perfect and so there are likely to be insecurities, mistakes and pain even as the new story is acted out. Lady Pastor is present with the cast, listening to the sound the cast is making. Without Lady Pastor being listened to and respected, the cast will find there are constant comings and goings amongst them and it might end up run like a business rather than function as a healthy community.

Sir Follower

Sir Follower is more important than he thinks. In the eyes of the Director, he is equal in standing to all members of the cast including Lady Pastor and Major Leader. It would be easy to allow other characters to make decisions, to decide the big story and to drive things forward. Sir Follower is free to speak out and challenge poor decisions and potentially abusive behaviours and practices. He should encourage and support the wonderful story being told but sometimes even the best stories need adjusting, adapting and editing as a result of honest feedback. The Director doesn't have a problem with questions, doubts about the plot line and concerns about those acting on his behalf. Sir Follower sometimes feels his voice is weak and unheard but when the culture is healthy, his voice is powerful and essential.

Ms Courageous

The whole cast needs to feel safe enough to make courageous decisions about themselves, their sphere of influence, their problems and challenges. It takes Ms Courage to do this but she is quite difficult to tie down and define. Sometimes Ms Courage is invisible and problematic to identify. Everyone can help by encouraging the whole team to speak out, share ideas and to give praise when Ms Courage has stepped out of her comfort zone. Courage grows when praised. Courage is sometimes supernatural. It is as though the Holy Spirit loves to provide strength. 'And Now, Let the Weak Say I Am Strong' will be sung over and over again. Ms Courage is not about doing something amazing, as for most the simple act of speaking out, challenging power or even sharing their story with a friend is courageous enough. Courage begins with a story told.

Major Leader

Major Leader has a difficult role to play. He often feels torn between two scripts, two ways of acting and two ways of saying the same thing. He has a responsibility to make decisions but also feels the need to ask others for their thoughts. He wants to get it right. Major Leader must be allowed to lead as that is his role but he must also be willing to tell the story of why he does what he does, admit to his mistakes and be very quick to apologise for his inevitable mistakes.

Major Leader sometimes goes off script but this is no bad thing as this is when the creative juices flow and ideas come. Major Leader is best when he is given the time, freedom and resources to have a go, without fearing personal attacks. Because Major Leader is often at the front, leading the way, some of the cast may feel a bit distant from him and not sure what is happening. Major Leader will make sure the cast knows where he is and what he is doing. There are no secrets. Major Leader will be very happy to step back and will make sure he is listening to and hearing the cast. He might hear things he doesn't like or that will mean he has to slow down but he learns that this is likely healthy and not a hindrance.

Dr Theology

Dr Theology shapes far more than many like to think. She loves to think, to read, to analyse and discover. Words are important and Dr Theology understands that thinking forms character and will eventually impact practice. Dr Theology will ask questions, not to find fault but to make sure that everyone is thinking well about themselves, others and God. The cast needs to listen well and be free to ask the toughest of questions. Dr Theology won't mind being asked and will love to give the best answers she can. She may not be right and will admit to her own uncertainties and live with mystery. Dr Theology doesn't try to impose her views but is able to help people discover answers for themselves based on good research, wise interpretation and different perspectives.

Ms Compassionate

The very nature or essence of the play being created is love, and so Ms Compassion is not an optional extra or the nice person in the corner. The whole cast smells of Ms Compassion. It is like she is everywhere in everything. Compassion motivates, drives, heals and acts. It is not just a feeling, but the power that enables the play to be seen and heard as a wonderful expression of grace and kindness. Without Ms Compassion, we have a religious play without feeling, bereft of power and lacking integrity. Ms Compassion is motivated by love; not some great plan to get people to think and act like her. She isn't trying to manipulate people to become part of the play. Ms Compassion loves because she is what she is.

Everyone Else

There are other characters that could be mentioned. It is a bit like the "thank you" speech that easily misses out important people and some of the audience will no doubt be quick to think, "What about him or her?" So let's be clear:

Everyone who is called into the script of this new story has a part to play and a responsibility to carry. It might be Mr Faith, Mrs Grace, Master Kindness, Miss Self-Control or numerous others. It is not a neat and tidy story and much has yet to be written. The beauty of the story depends on everyone fulfilling their role and living under the direction of the Director. It is not about the leader or the follower, but about both mingling together as both recognise that every part is important. The Director prays:

"I am not praying for the world, but for those You have given Me, for they are Yours. All I have is Yours, and all You have is Mine. And glory has come to Me through them. I will remain in the world no longer, but they are still in the world, and I am coming to You. Holy Father, protect them by the power of Your name, the name You gave Me, so that they may be one as We are One. While I was with them, I protected them and kept them safe by that name You gave Me" (John 17:9–12).

The new story will move beyond the worn-out leadership theories, will reject simplistic and dangerous theological answers and re-think mistaken concepts about followers being less important than leaders. If leadership and followership are separated from one another, there will be more appalling stories to tell. Healthy, fearless, safe churches are rooted in wise theology. "The beginning of wisdom is this: Get wisdom" (Proverbs 4:7). The focus of the new story that must be told is culture and we all help create this. Yes, leadership as a function is vitally important but so is followership and so are you! When we are one, the church becomes the safe, fearless community it is designed to be.

At this point, let me say a little about leadership in the church. It is a joy and privilege to be called into any leadership role. Reducing the gaps between leader and follower and demolishing the hierarchies does not mean leadership is unimportant. Leadership in all its complexity and forms is essential. But with any leadership role (in whatever church system you are constrained by), comes leadership responsibility and it is the team leader that will set the tone and be the catalyst to creating healthy cultures. Courageous followers have the power to make the leadership role safer and wiser. Courageous leaders will encourage their team and their church to be the courageous followers that safe, fearless churches need.

DAVID WARREN

Encore

Great stories usually end with loose ends being tied up, solutions found or the suspect finally arrested. Great concerts end with an encore where there is a crescendo of applause. Great sports events end with presentations, chants and parties. The end of this story (my story and the stories of everyone and everything) is a crescendo of beauty even if right now it feels to some readers it remains a story of pain. Your story has not ended! The resurrection of Jesus shouts out that there is always hope and this hope will not disappoint.

One day two men were walking towards Emmaus. Once they were full of hope but now hope had gone. The one who had been their "everything" and the "everything" to so many of their friends and family had been cruelly and unjustly killed. As they walked and talked a man drew alongside. He listened and proceeded to share the story of the history of their people. They wanted to hear more, so asked the stranger to stay and eat. Bread and wine were shared, eyes were opened and hope returned. Jesus was with them and very much alive. Shalom be with you!

If you are a leader who struggles with any of the behaviour patterns we have talked about, Jesus is the "everything" you need to change. He gives courage.

If you have been subject to abuse of any kind, Jesus can be the "everything" you need to heal. He gives courage.

If you are suffering from abusive behaviours of any kind, Jesus is the "everything" you need, but please talk to someone you trust. He gives courage.

If you are a Christ-follower and desire to be part of the answer, then Jesus is the everything you need to speak out, challenge and encourage change. He gives courage.

If you are a leader who wants to be a catalyst for change and healthy cultural development, then Jesus is the "everything" you need to be wise in word and deed. He gives courage.

A safe and fearless church doesn't just happen and it is all too easy to think that this new story should be nice and comfortable. It isn't. It won't be. It can't be. We are all in a battle and behind the scenes there are the unseen powers of a VUCA world that will attempt to drag us down and do us harm. We must all remind ourselves that this battle is not one of flesh and blood but a spiritual war that has already been won through servanthood, suffering, cross and resurrection. Jesus is on the throne.

Consider this:

"Every act of love, gratitude, and kindness; every work of art or music inspired by the love of God and delight in the beauty of his creation; every minute spent teaching a severely handicapped child to read

or to walk; every act of care and nurture, of comfort and support, for one's fellow human beings and for that matter, one's fellow non-human creatures; and of course every prayer, all Spirit-led teaching, every deed that spreads the Gospel, builds up the church, embraces and embodies holiness rather than corruption, and makes the name of Jesus honoured in the world — all of this will find its way, through the resurrecting power of God, into the new creation that God will one day make. That is the logic of the mission of God. God's recreation of His wonderful world, which began with the resurrection of Jesus and continues mysteriously as God's people live in the risen Christ and in the power of His Spirit, means that what we do in Christ and by the Spirit in the present is not wasted. It will last all the way into God's new world. In fact, it will be enhanced there."
— N.T. Wright, 'Surprised by Hope: Rethinking Heaven, the Resurrection, and the Mission of the Church'

DAVID WARREN

Part Four:
Jesus Shaped Culture

We have heard the stories, sought out some potential answers and been challenged to be part of a new story that must be written. It is time to go back to where we began the book — back to the one who saw "everything", listened to "everything" and then cast out all fear. Perfect Love (Jesus) casts out all fear. The themes of courageous followership, psychological safety and wise theology are all wrapped up in Jesus. But firstly, and very briefly, we need to say something about leadership and the loud voices that attempt to divert attention away from Jesus.

DAVID WARREN

Leadership and Culture

I am reminded of a story (it may be apocryphal) of a group who gathered together in a home in those early charismatic days I spoke of in my story. They were struggling and beginning to argue as they attempted to resist any form of human control as their desire was to be led only by the Holy Spirit. They sought out advice and a wise person asked this question: "Who are the sheep bleating at?" The response was overwhelming and a leader emerged. The one to whom the sheep were bleating was leading, had influence and was respected. Where there's no clarity of leadership and no structures, leaders will inevitably emerge or chaos will reign. There are, of course, different definitions, viewpoints, structures and titles for leadership in the church but the culture of any church will inevitably reflect the leadership of that community. Wise, safe, fearless leaders will create wise, safe, fearless cultures. Leadership is important.

We have recognised that the dynamic relationship between leader and follower has changed and continues to change. Followers are more important and perhaps more powerful than ever before, but leaders are still the ones who create the cultures where followers can function in the courageous way we have highlighted. Courageous followership only emerges where there is secure leadership. With this in mind, we must complete our journey with a look into church leadership in the light of Jesus. As Ken

Blanchard wrote, "The more I read the Bible, the more evident it becomes that everything I have ever taught or written about effective leadership over the past 25 years, Jesus did it to perfection. He is simply the greatest leadership role model of all time."[15]

Voices That Challenge

'The Voice' is a talent show where at the initial audition the judges are seated facing away from the performer. They cannot see what the nervous performer looks like or dresses like. The voice of the image is silenced by the real voice. If they like what they hear, they turn and face the person behind the voice. Leaders choose the voices they turn to look at and choose to be influenced by. Some voices are extremely attractive, compelling and very powerful but move us away from the voice of Jesus. These are the voices of Babylon.

"Looking back, I (David) have realised some of the practices I've been involved with and supported, were in fact, very unlike Jesus' leadership. On one occasion I was involved with VIP lounges, hiring cars to transport VIPs short distances from hotel to venue, roping off VIP front seats and an extravagant green room hospitality lounge. I saw internationally well-known speakers make demands and speak to those who were serving as slaves rather than brothers and sisters. On one occasion this meant a staircase could only be used by the elite. All of this was done in the name of generosity whilst volunteers served for hours and attendees were asked to give more of their finances. At the time I enjoyed it all, but now realise that it created an unhealthy culture where leaders are separate and more important than the rest. Jesus did not seem to like 'top tables!'"

The beautiful voices of honour, respect and generosity are too easily silenced by hierarchy, power, extravagance and mates' clubs. What looks good, sounds good and in many ways is good, can create distraction and a sense of "us and them" that seeps into the culture.

I've always had a heart for the poor and have tried to create churches where we serve the community around us without motive, nor for personal or corporate gain. We serve because we serve. The voice of the poor is heard but sadly there are times when the cry is used to promote the voice of the church. When leaders make the poor a means to advertise their church, then we have turned the voice of the poor into the dangerous voice of advertising and an attractive brand. We begin to use our God-given financial and human resources as a kind of advertising agency. The beautiful voice of the poor is twisted and easily becomes the voice of strangled humility and image management.

"When I was in my new role, I discovered a new job in church: show-caller. I have never quite understood it but gathered it was all about making sure the service ('show' as some called it) went according to a very precise and planned schedule. Every minute had to be accounted for, and the lectern had to appear on the stage at just the right time. The music played as the appeal took place, was of a certain key and all aspects were tightly controlled including the image of those on stage."

The voice of performance is very strong and, in some

ways, valid. Why not look good and sound good? If it helps people to stay and provides something exciting and professional to invite people to, what could be wrong? Tacky, poor-quality sound, lighting and heating can really put folks off. I am reminded of the dreadfully typed notice sheet and my first brave attempts at publicity. It was often embarrassing. I am also aware of the extraordinary Cathedrals, Abbeys and the like that were built with beauty, majesty and the performance of ritual in mind. The theatre of religious performance is nothing new. The problem comes when the performance becomes so important that people are rejected because they don't clap, can't jump, wear the wrong style clothes or are too old to be seen on the stage of the young. People are "othered" and performance standards are used as a measure of success and an anointed meeting. The voice of performance also creates the personality, the Christian stage star which in turn feeds egos and the need to do better next time.

Most of us are caught up in a success narrative of one form or another. We must sell more, create more, grow more, achieve more and create more profit. We have shareholders to satisfy, bosses to please, systems to keep going. Success is largely a numbers game. The bios of many Christian conference speakers and pastors speak of the voice of success. "Pastor George's church has grown from 50 to over 4000 and he is about to embark on a project to build a 2500 seat auditorium." If success is measured by numbers, then culture will be driven by numbers and health will be measured by numbers. Faith goals (targets) sneak in the backdoor and stories emerge of stress and fear if the goals are not reached. If we work harder, give more time, create better programmes, all will be well and we can go to the next leadership conference, the next leadership team meeting, the next one-to-one with the senior leader confident that when the inevitable numbers question is asked, we can say we are growing or the giving has gone up! I do not know of one pastor who doesn't want their church to reach more people and see more lives transformed, but the voice of "Well done, good and faithful servant" is so easily drowned out by the Babylonian voice of twenty-first century success. Numbers and achievement are the breeding ground for pride and fertile soil for narcissism to flourish. The large crowd and the grand vision are often associated with a lack of accountability, burnout of followers and fragile, shallow discipleship. As the 2024 Landmark Chamber's report into the Soul Survivor states, "Overarching all this is the view we've taken that, when an organisation is seen as successful, people do not look carefully enough about what the price may be for such success." When we hear the voice of numbers as the voice of success, we are looking at the wrong person on the stage!

Jesus loved people, but was often angered by those who fostered a religious system that protected itself rather than protecting the widow and the orphan — hypocrites, blind guides, fools, white sepulchres and vipers. The voice of protection shouts: We must be careful what we say, how we respond, what we look like. Our image, our brand and therefore our people, will be damaged. The body of Christ needs us to protect it from harm! There is, of course, truth in this. Why shoot ourselves in the foot? Why not do all we can to make sure the world speaks well of us? The trouble is that the voice of reputation begins to speak more loudly than the voice of Jesus.

Churches employ reputation companies rather than admit to mistakes and the stories of cover ups begin to emerge. If Jesus is the head of the Church, if Jesus reigns and rules, if Jesus is building His Church and the gates of hell will not prevail, if Jesus is coming back to claim a beautiful Bride, then why are we often more concerned with our reputation than with the image-bearing people whom Jesus came to heal, set free and whom ultimately will be part of the beautiful new creation reality? We are not called to shepherd an institution, we are called to shepherd people.

DAVID WARREN

Jesus: Wise, Safe and Courageous

At the centre of all the stories of pain, love, sadness, joy, hope, kindness, abuse and painful experiences stands Jesus. He was in it from the beginning and will be in it at the end. We may not understand His ways, nor do some feel His presence or currently follow His path. Those that have been abused and harmed by the actions of the church of which Jesus is head, often find it tough (if not impossible) to reconcile their experiences with the life and teaching of Christ.

So, I finish this book by placing Christ centre-stage, as Director of the story and plead the case for the church and especially its leaders to listen to this voice, turn their chairs and face Him. Let The Voice resound by listening again to the words and thoughts of Matthew, Mark, Luke and John who walked the walk, heard the stories and experienced the fearless love of Christ before writing their story of the good news of the Kingdom of peace, righteousness, joy and hope that comes to earth as it is in heaven. Wise, safe, fearless Christlike leadership is:

- Humility and selflessness. These are the qualities of true greatness.
    - "Whoever wants to be My disciple must deny themselves and take up their cross and follow Me" (Matthew 16:24).

- Jesus said, "For even the Son of Man did not come to be served, but to serve, and to give His life as a ransom for many" (Mark 10:45).

- Judas betrayed Jesus for 30 pieces of silver and He knew it would happen. Astonishingly Matthew and John tell us that Jesus still washed the feet of Judas and fed him at the last supper. Jesus loved and cared for Judas despite his evil intentions. He lived the words, "Do unto others as you would have them do unto you."

- Compassion for the weak and care for the poor. "His yoke is easy and His burden light" (Matthew 11:30).

  - But Jesus looked out at the crowds and "had compassion on them and healed their sick" (Matthew 14:14). Jesus felt compassion because the people were "weary and worn out, like sheep without a shepherd" (Matthew: 9:35–37).

- Stewardship and accountability to God and others for actions and words. "From everyone who has been given much, much will be demanded; and from the one who has been entrusted with much, much more will be asked" (Luke 12:48).

  - If we are to build safe, fearless church

cultures, every Christian leader must lead with The Voice ringing in their ears.

- No more words are needed. It is over to you and me. We must be, can be and are so much better than we've been. Let's turn our chairs and face Jesus.

DAVID WARREN

Conclusion

A good story ends with a sense of satisfaction. Problems are solved, the murderer is revealed or Dogger is found. Some stories end with the sense that there will be the inevitable sequel or a new tale to tell.

I hope this book has finished on a high (Jesus) but also sets us up for the new. There is much to learn and more exciting adventures to experience. There will be ups and downs and mistakes will inevitably be made. It is, after all, a very human story! If we act out our new story with wise theology, psychological safety, courageous followership and with our eyes focused on Jesus, it will be a story that shines light into dark places and creates healthy, vibrant church cultures where "othering" is banished and everything and everyone shouts "this is the beautiful Bride of Christ!"

That is my prayer.

DAVID WARREN

References

[1] Russell L., Long, M. & Harrison, P. 'Pioneer Trust Safeguarding Learning Review: Full Report'. Christian Safeguarding Services (2024), Pp. 1–76. https://pioneer.org.uk/wp-content/uploads/2024/05/Pioneer-Trust-Review.pdf

[2] See Pew Research Center 2010 report: pewresearch.org

[3] Wright, N.T. Scripture and the Authority of God: How To Read the Bible Today. (HarperOne: 2013).

[4] I am indebted to a paper by Samuel Pfeifer M.D. entitled, 'Mental Health and Christian Ministry' in Doon Theological Journal 11.2 (2014) p. 144–155, for some of the ideas here.

[5] Langberg, D. 'Redeeming Power: Understanding Authority and Abuse in the Church'. BrazosPress (2020), p. 93.

[6] See especially Amy C. Edmondson. 'The Fearless Organisation'. Wiley. 2018.

[7] Maxwell. J. C. 'The 21 Indisputable Qualities of a Leader'. (Nashville, Thomas Nelson. 1999. p.xi.).

[8] Ricketson. R. 'Follower First: Rethinking Leading in the Church'. Miami Beach: Heartworks, Publications (2009), p. 39.

[9] Kelly, R. E. 'Rethinking Followership in the Art of

Followership'. Jossey-Bass. San Francisco (2008), p.11.

[10] Banks R. & Ledbetter B. M. 'Reviewing Leadership: A Christian Evaluation of Current Leadership Approaches'. Grand Rapids: Baker Academic (2004), p. 38.

[11] Sweet, L. 'I am a Follower: The Way, The Truth, and Life of Following Jesus'. Louisville: Thomas Nelson (2012), p. 23.

[12] Chalef, I. 'The Courageous Follower: Standing Up to and for Our Leaders'. Oakwood: Barrett-Koehler (1995).

[13] Kelly, R. E. 'The Power of Followership: How to Create Leaders People Want to Follow and Followers Who Lead Themselves'. Doubleday, New York, (1992).

[14] McKnight, S. & Matchett, C. 'Revelation for the Rest of Us'. Zondervan Reflective (2023).

[15] Blanchard, K. & Hodges, P. 'Lead Like Jesus'. Nashville, TN, Thomas Nelson, (2008).

About the Author

David Warren has been a church leader in various roles and settings for over 40 years. He has taught in primary and secondary schools in the United Kingdom and has a Master's Degree in Missional Leadership. He is married with three grown up children and three little grandchildren. Now retired David loves all sport and can often be found playing indoor bowls (badly).

DAVID WARREN

About PublishU

PublishU enables you to tell your story or communicate your message by writing and publishing a book worldwide.

"I never thought I would be able to write a book, let alone in 100 days... now I'm asking what else have I told myself that I can't do that I actually can?'"

PublishU Author

To find out more visit

www.PublishU.com

DAVID WARREN

Printed in Dunstable, United Kingdom